OBSESSED

Gimmick Press Presents

OBSESSED

Essays on Pop Culture Obsession

OBSESSED: Essays on Pop Culture Obsession

Published by Gimmick Press

Cover art and layout by Katie MacDonald

GimmickPress.com

ISBN: 978-1-0878-9286-3

Table of Contents

Dr. Benjamin Anthony
Animal Obsessions: The Allure of Animal Crossing 1

J. A. Bernstein
On the Most Magical Kiss in the History of Hollywood 9

Michael Chin
Waiting In Line to Meet Wrestlers 14

Maggie Dove
She Wears The Batman 27

Jacob Fowler
An Elegy for the King of Parodies 40

Madeline Lane-McKinley
A Love Letter to Pee-Wee 46

Charles Austin Muir
Lost in a Debbie Gibson Music Video 54

Mark A. Nobles
Tom Cruise Can Kiss My Ass 67

Josh Olsen
To BUNT, or not to BUNT 74

Matt Springer
Time to Match the Stars 80

Kyle Stedman
Drenched in 1988 86

Adam Van Winkle
Wrestling on TV, Wrestling with the Past 110

Tom G. Wolf
Adventures in Paranormal Publishing 117

Contributors 127

DR. BENJAMIN ANTHONY
Animal Obsessions: The Allure of Animal Crossing

Five years ago, I could not count the number of people on my twitter timeline obsessing about something called Animal Crossing: New Leaf. Being a mid-thirties dad to a young girl who was already obsessed with her Nintendo, I looked into the game and found a seemingly simple game about being the mayor of a town full of talking animals. We went to the local video game store and plunked down the thirty dollars and came home with a brand-new copy of Animal Crossing: New Leaf.

At the time my daughter was only five years old, but she was fully immersed into the game as we played together. She was the mayor of course, naming her town Pickles and logging thousands of hours picking fruit, catching fish, digging holes and chopping down trees. Your actions in the game unlock additional features, expanded areas to investigate, new characters to interact with and items to buy and sell. My initial feelings were that the game was fun, but I couldn't imagine it holding my daughter's attention for too long, she's incredibly active, constantly running around, chasing her dog, catching real bugs, drawing pictures and playing with her friends. I gave the game three months before she grew disinterested in it and moved on to another cartridge.

It's now five years later, she still plays Animal Crossing: New Leaf nearly every day, her town is filled with special projects she has built and has been landscaped to the exacting details of all my little girl's wishes. Her home in the game has gone from a tiny pup tent to a large mansion with multiple rooms, filled with all sorts of furniture and decorations. The villagers in her town have come and gone, some moving out, while some she refuses to let leave, talking to them every day so that they can't move away. See, if you don't interact with say Bobby the horse for several weeks, he will move away to someplace else and a new animal will replace him. The game takes place in real time as well, so every hour that passes in real life is an hour in the game. There is a way to time travel, which creates problems all its own, though it does offer advantages for unscrupulous mayors.

New Leaf is the fourth game in the Animal Crossing series, the first coming out in 2001 for the Nintendo Game Cube, followed by Animal Crossing: Wild World coming out on the DS and Animal Crossing: City Folk which was on the Wii. All of the games follow a similar pattern of living in a town and interacting with animal characters, spending time fishing, digging up fossils, picking fruit, planting flowers, buying and selling items at the assorted stores in the game.

The simplicity of the game play would not lead most people to think that it is one of the most popular games from Nintendo, or that it would inspire such ravenous fans. But both these things are true. A recent Nintendo Direct, where release dates for new games are announced, led to a twitter storm when no actual date was put forth for the next installment in the series on the Nintendo Switch. Fans were apocalyptic, suicidal, despondent and enraged, screaming for news of the next Animal Crossing title, which has been confirmed for release in 2019, though no specific date has been given. Only a short video has been released, which does not include any game play footage or hints of what new features will be in the game. By the time this sees print the new Animal Crossing game will be up for pre-order or even available for purchase, so take this as a cry from the past, from a father who listens constantly to his daughter asking when will the game be here? Why haven't they said when it is coming out? When? Why? God help me if the game is delayed or, heaven forbid, canceled.

Why? Such a big question for three short letters. Why would a simple game about doing daily chores with talking animals inspire such devotion and obsession? I can't guarantee a conclusive answer, but I'm going to suggest some ideas that might help you reach an answer.

First, of course, the game is a form of escapism. Every day in the real world we are surrounded by negative things, people arguing over politics, deaths, disease, job stresses, school stresses, money problems, weather disasters and the myriad other problems in life. All these things affect all of us from childhood to adulthood to old age, of course in varying degrees, but no one can escape the knowledge of all the suffering and problems in the world. The problems in Animal Crossing are nearly non-existent. Getting stung by a swarm of bees, about the worst thing that can happen, merely leads to a slightly swollen face for a day, which every villager will comment on. Medicine is available at the store to remedy the bee stings though, so even that is not a real problem. Sharks are creatures in the game as well, but swimming near them merely makes them swim away, there is no danger of them attacking while you swim around in the ocean. Jellyfish can sting you as well, but like the stings from a swarm of bees, there is no real danger in being stung by them.

Villagers can move away from the town, though invariably they will appear again in the shopping district, say hello and talk wistfully about their time living in your town. The main obstacle in the game seems to be paying off home expansion loans, as when you first have your home built it is a small one room building, barely big enough for a bed and night-stand. Once the loan to the local Realtor, Tom Nook (a greedy raccoon) is paid off you can expand your house, again taking out a loan which must be repaid before more expansions can be built. Though unlike real life, there is no time limit, or fees for late payments. Tom Nook will happily accept all the bells (bells are the currency in Animal Crossing) that you give him, though there is no penalties if you never pay back a cent of your home loan. There is no foreclosure system in Animal Crossing, no sheriff's auction when you fail to pay your property taxes, no IRS threatening to garnish your wages or debt collectors blowing up your phone with threats of reporting you to collection agencies. There's no crime in Animal Crossing, unless not talking to a village is considered a crime. It's a peaceful world that lets you come and go as you please, a complete difference from all the headaches of the real world.

The second thing about the game is that it is funny. Villagers talk in weird ways, ask you to do trivial things for them and reward you with furniture, wallpaper or other gifts. For example, one day I ran into Fang the wolf, and he told me how he was just dying to eat an apple. Now mere steps away from the both of us was a grove of apple trees, ripe for the picking. So, I walked over, shook an apple tree and three apples fell to the ground. I picked them up and went back over to Fang, gave him one and he thanked me profusely, giving me a couch in his gratitude for me walking a few steps away and picking up an apple. Other villagers will tell you jokes or ask you to find them missing items, which are usually laying on the ground around their house.

The game is engrossing. Every day something different is going on, from holidays and birthdays to visits from the art dealer, the fortune teller or turnip seller, something always seems to be happening. Though no actions are really required, as mayor of the town you are free to roam around and do as you please. If you just want to spend a day fishing on the beach it's totally fine! You have an assistant in the mayor's office, Isabelle, who takes care of organizing all activities and events. As mayor there are no expectations of you. When new villagers move into town and first meet you, they will gush and talk about what an honor it is to meet the mayor. Though the more effort you put into completing tasks and interacting with the assorted villagers and shopkeepers the more you will be rewarded with additional content and interesting areas to explore.

Now as to some of the obsessions with the game, there are of course a whole line of plush toys, miniature figures, t-shirts, stickers, Amiibo figures to wirelessly interact with your Nintendo products, comics and posters, there's even a movie that is on YouTube if you search for it. With the release of the next installment in the game I think we will witness an overwhelming number of new fans of the Animal Crossing series and I will of course be buying all the assorted trinkets and toys as my daughter requests. Though of course some of this whole business of obsession with Animal Crossing leads to some existential questions for dads (and moms too, of course).

Why do we buy all this stuff? How long are our kids really going to play with these things? How can we put a price on our children's happiness? Aren't we just perpetuating the cycle of consumerism by giving in to every obsession our children develop? How can we tell them that no, buying more blind bags filled with plastic figures is not what they really need without causing a scene in the toy store? Even if we convince them that buying more toys is not the path to happiness, what do we tell them is the path to happiness? Does saving money for a down payment on a house or to pay off credit card debt really lead to more enjoyment of life? When do we introduce our children to the concept of the free market and its mortal enemy socialism?

Thankfully Animal Crossing provides a gentle introduction to answering many of these questions. How? After so long playing the game you inevitably reach a point where you have more things than space for those things and you have to start making choices. Do you need every pattern and color of wallpaper, every different style of couch, or can you live with just your favorite things? Do you want to just focus on getting things for yourself or do you want to put your money towards projects that the other villagers would like? A bridge or a beautiful statue can bring joy to the other villagers, where expanding your own house is just going to make you happier. What sort of mayor do you want to be, one that increases the prices on everything in town or one that makes a town ordinance that everyone should keep their property clear of weeds?

Beneath the simple exterior, the Animal Crossing games gently nudge players towards the joy of creating a community and sense of belonging. Maybe that is the real secret to why they are so popular? Players can visit other towns and send messages to each other, go fishing together or just hang out in the aquarium admiring all the fish and sea creatures they have collected. There are no wrong answers or wrong ways to play the game. The goalposts of the game are almost non-existent, there is no ending, or winning the game, it is just something that you can play and enjoy without feeling like you need to do something else, or that you are missing out.

Speaking of missing out, there are time related events, and the afore-mentioned ability to time travel in the game. The advantages of course are that you never have to miss an event. You wanted to make it to Fang's birthday party but overtime at work got the better of you? No problem, just go back in time to his birthday, present in hand, and no one is the wiser. Want to watch the Fourth of July fireworks celebration again? Just go back in time to that day and watch pixels explode on your screen to your heart's content. If you've deposited bells in the bank, interest will accumulate while you are away, which is where unscrupulous mayors can bend the rules, or in effect, hack the game.

The disadvantage is that if you time travel too much, weeds will overtake your town, and people will think you have left for however long you traveled back and forth. Some might have even moved away in your perceived absence. Since you have been traveling in time, and not spending time in your house, bugs may have moved in as well, which while not a problem, can be embarrassing. As with the rest of the game play in Animal Crossing though, all problems are relatively minor and easily surmounted by spending some time talking to the other villagers and performing basic chores like picking weeds.

Animal Crossing is a fun game, no doubt about it, one that is deceptively simple but actually is completely engrossing. In the five years that my daughter and I have been playing it, we've never gotten tired of the game and are just as eager as the rest of the fans for the next release. I've spent countless dollars on Amiibo and plush toys, and honestly have no problem with the next small fortune to be spent once the new game is released. If that isn't obsession, then I don't know what is.

If you do decide to visit Animal Crossing, then be sure to look up my town, the town of Booty.

J. A. BERNSTEIN
On the Most Magical Kiss in the History of Hollywood

Allow me to wax sentimental for a moment about a woman of late-Eighties lore, a one Ellen Reed, who marked the fictional love interest—before she was horridly replaced—of Alex P. Keaton (Michael J. Fox) on the Reagan-era favorite, *Family Ties*. Ellen was portrayed by Tracy Pollan, who would later become an actress of some repute and end up wedding Fox several years later. Anyone who had eyes and ears in the mid-Eighties, however, and avidly watched the show, as I did, can recall that whenever Ellen stepped onto the set, there was a peculiar awkwardness to her, a kind of visceral shyness, combined with an air of self-possession, that made it more than abundantly clear that this relationship wasn't just screened.

Put aside for a second the premise of the series: that Keaton, a blazer-sporting, *Wall Street Journal*-toting Reaganite, who routinely kisses a mounted photograph of Nixon himself before heading off to bed—this was at the height of Iran-Contra Era, mind you—could fall in love with an unabashed feminist and artist, as Ellen claimed to be. Also try to disregard what Ellen normally wore: the standard-issue, shoulder-padded dress or huge cable-knit sweater, complemented by tortoiseshell glasses, front-parted bangs, and the requisite smidgens of rouge. Finally, forget for a moment that the show always ended with a sappy and heartwarming sermon about the importance of filial bonds—or family ties, as the show rightfully called itself (and which sounds like the name of a bad porn flic).

All obstructions aside, Ellen, the first time she set foot on the series, left me in a veritable trance. There was something so captivating about her, so stirring and raw, in spite of all the makeup and gloss: the fact that her nose was slightly misaligned, as mine is; that her flaxen brown hair, while lacking the glow of Tina Yothers', among others', still had a hint of goyishness to it, and a convincing one at that; that her lips, which were almost eternally pursed, as if in confusion or dismay that she'd be dating a Republican—or, worse, find herself smitten by him, as she evidently was—looked superhuman and outdid the most scandalous Guess ad; and most of all her eyes, a kind of periwinkle blue that, in retrospect, seemed almost characteristic of the late-Eighties: less bright than the vivid sky blue of Kelly LeBrock or the heady azure of Kim Basinger and more akin to the glowing maze inside *Pac-Man*. There was something entirely quieting about her: the softness of her face, combined with the rigidness of her stare, her perpetual air of self-confidence, and the way you knew, well before Season 5, that they would split, that she was way too good for this imbecile, even if she'd reduce herself later.

Indeed, might I confess that this was probably the first moment in my life when I was irretrievably in love? I was all of seven-years-old, and the show premiered Thursday nights at eight-thirty, well past my second-grade bedtime. Like many middle-class Americans growing up in the mid-to-late Eighties, however, I was blessed to have my own television—an old Zenith set that, in retrospect, probably rivaled the width of my family's Maxima station wagon and, come to think of it, could not have revealed her blue eyes, and yet, somehow, tangibly, *did*.

Today, in the age of color television—not to mention digital, God help us—we forget what it means to see blue eyes along a screen: the way they can shimmer so starkly, especially in black-and-white. I even recall, eerily enough, how the shade of her eyes matched the shade of her dress and, later, those horrendous, blue cable-knit sweaters. I can't recall a word that she said on the series—or what anyone else said, for that matter, which is less a testament to the drabness of its screenwriting than my own limited powers of recall. Still, I do recall the moment when Alex and Ellen first kissed: midway through the second episode, when they were seated along a bench in a smoky train station and Ellen had confessed she was engaged to another man.

Wikipedia tells me that the date was October 3, 1985. Gorbachev was still in office, the Cold War then in full swing. Earlier that summer, *Back to the Future* had premiered, catapulting Fox to fame, and that very morning, the space shuttle *Atlantis* had successfully reached outer space—this was months before the *Challenger* would sputter and plume through the sky, taking with it, it would seem, the whole of Generation X's collective and unbridled innocence.

But *would* she stay with him? After all, Dennis, Ellen's college-aged suitor, and to whom she was apparently betrothed, obviously boasted good standing. (Though ask yourself: could he wire a flux capacitor?) When Ellen, about to leave the station and return to her fiancé, slowly turned around, approached Alex, and nuzzled her face into his, then softly, effervescently kissed him, the entire fucking world stood still.

Yes, I had seen kisses before. I would even endure a few, painfully, in middle school, mostly on account of a dare. But I had never before—and probably never have since—encountered a kiss of That Magnitude.

In some ways, it could only occur on a show with conservative, Reaganesque values, one where the lead character dons a Brooks Brothers tie and combs his hair neatly in a part—not unlike a youthful P. J. O'Rourke, in fact. Even Ellen, upon leaving Alex once more, turns to look at him stoically, her bangs still aglow, her hands meekly folded in his, and watches him with a kind of knowingness, a sort of *I'm better than you, motherfucker, and I'll put up with all of your preppy ass shit, even your leaving me for Courtney Cox, because I am what makes you. I am your fucking bride to be* kind of look.

Whether the two ever dated on-set is unknown, though Fox and Pollan would end up marrying in '88, apparently the result of meeting once again on the set of *Bright Lights, Big City*. Those of us who watched the series, though—who witnessed The Kiss, a kind of miracle-embrace of borderline Klimtian proportions—well knew that this couple was destined to be together, regardless of what the screenwriters thought.

Of course, their romance is only compounded and now heightened by the fact that Fox suffers from Parkinson's. Pollen herself hasn't aged too well, either. Her face looks a little bit sculpted, to put it bluntly. But who can blame her after having four kids, much less coping with Marty McFly? Still, for all his flaws, I'm infinitely jealous of the man and eternally grateful to the show for having imbued me with the lessons of love, chief among them the knowledge that all beauty is fleeting but really fucking great while it lasts. Oh, and it turns out the Baby Boomers were unrepentant capitalists, despite what Alex Keaton thought. But I guess that's another ordeal.

MICHAEL CHIN
Waiting In Line to Meet Wrestlers

There are only three professional wrestlers I've called my favorite.

Child of the eighties, did I ever stand a chance against Hulk Hogan's bulging-bicep, flag-waving-overhead, giant-slamming persona?

Right hand right hand right hand Irish whip big boot leg drop.

Who could resist falling?

My next favorite was Razor Ramon.

In the cloud of a post-Hulkamania world, I saw the vignettes of him riding with the top down and flicking toothpicks in the faces of lesser men.

Though these cinematic preview clips of Scott Hall aping Scarface have become a part of his legend, I didn't feel a connection until I saw him in the ring. That debut match, I was in awe of this big bully of a man, and in particular the Razor's Edge crucifix powerbomb that requires such strength and looked so brutal.

A live event, Utica Memorial Auditorium, 1993, my father won floor seats on a radio call-in show. When Ramon's music hit, he urged me to go closer to the railing and to hold out my hand. I understood wrestling wasn't real—Dad had made sure I knew from as early as I can remember.

Still, I understood bad guys didn't slap hands with fans, and despite my father's insistence that maybe he would this time, I only went so far as to stand up closer to the railing to get a better look at him as he walked by.

A year or so later, Razor Ramon came back to Utica, and though he went by the moniker "The Bad Guy," he had in fact become one of the top good guys in wrestling by that point—so much so that he was scheduled for an autograph appearance at Pizza Hut.

Dad drove my best friend Mike from down the street and I to the signing. He was taking us to the WWF show that night, too, all of which I read as a matter of debt repayment, for it was I who usually hung out at my friend's house after school and I who had been the guest there for dinner multiple times, none of which I then (or now) saw as an imposition. Nonetheless, my friend's family seemed to recognize Dad taking their son to the show as their own debt, thus sending Mike with extra cash to pay for our concessions at not only the show, but the Pizza Hut, too, which made a small killing in Personal Pan Pizzas and cheesy bread to kids waiting to meet their idol that day.

It hadn't entered my mind how long the wait would be to meet Ramon, but when we arrived, not an hour after school let out, right at the time when the signing was to begin, we found ourselves already staring at a line that snaked out of the restaurant, curled around the perimeter of the parking lot. Ramon was not so much as visible from our position in line, and the line only grew behind us.

An hour into our wait, I don't think it had occurred to me that we wouldn't actually get to meet Ramon. After all, we already had our promotional black and white, glossy eight by tens of Ramon in hand. We'd already waited so long. The line had moved and surely, in the end, we'd get there.

What I didn't know then, what I'd read in the autobiography of Ramon's contemporary, Bret Hart, published some fifteen years later, was that Ramon was notorious for skipping out on signings, regardless of how long fans had waited. In a particularly villainous instance, Hart recalled Ramon leaving a young fan waiting for an autograph before ghosting on him altogether, claiming he didn't need to do that stuff anymore, the implication from Hart's eyes that Ramon saw himself as a big enough star that didn't have to be decent to individual fans anymore.

We did not meet Ramon that day. Two and a half hours of waiting, and we left. All we had to show for it were stomachs sick from the pepperoni pizza we'd bought in line, the edges of our eight by tens crumpled at the edges from where we'd gripped them tight in anticipation.

Truth be told, Razor Ramon wasn't really my favorite wrestler anyway by the time I stood in line to meet him.

January 1993, Ramon had challenged new WWF Champion Bret "The Hitman" Hart for his title at the Royal Rumble pay per view, and I had my first glimmer of the internal conflict that comes with cheering for a villain. Because, yes, I thought Ramon was cool and the Razor's Edge captured my imagination. But if Ramon were someone to look up to, Hart was someone I could relate to. He was an underdog, relegated to the tag team and middle of the card ranks up until he got his big break. And when he won the world title, he didn't come across as a reimagined super hero, but rather as a fighting champion who'd refuse to quit and find clever ways of overcoming obstacles that, on paper, should have been beyond him.

I still told my father Ramon was my favorite, because that was the way of our family, one foot in, one foot out of the realities and stories of wrestling. He'd made sure from an early age that I understood the fix was in, and what happened on TV was more staged performance than sport. Simultaneously, he'd dismiss smaller wrestlers like Hart and Shawn Michaels and The 1-2-3 Kid because it was laughable they'd stand a chance in a fight against the larger likes of Ramon, Bam Bam Bigelow, or Yokozuna.

In my heart of hearts, though, I saw myself in The Hitman.

I was in my late twenties when I got the chance to meet Bret Hart. Probably too old to be standing in line to meet a wrestler, and yet the culture had changed, too. Geeking out was in and after playing my wrestling obsession close to the vest through college and the years to immediately follow, even only cluing my first live-in girlfriend to a limited extent that watching Monday Night Raw was a guilty pleasure—I came out full throttle.

So it was that two guys from the office shared with me their own fanhood from their youths and came to me to talk about what was going on in contemporary wrestling. So it was that one of them alerted me Hart would be signing autographs at a minor league baseball game a mile from his house, out in the sticks, an hour drive from where we worked.

We went to the game after work, casually buying hotdogs and Miller Lites from the concession stand before the three of us assumed our place in line.

Before we realized the magnitude of the line.

Before we realized how slow the line was moving.

Wait in a long enough line, and you start to do the math. That a minor league baseball stadium is only so large, and the line hadn't wrapped around and doubled up on itself. A half hour and we might be behind the home team dugout. An hour and surely, we'd be able to see The Hitman, if only at a distance. An hour and a half, two hours tops we'd meet him.

I felt a twinge of guilt at subjecting my friends to this excursion, because surely it was only out of loyalty to me, or some deep-seated sense of not leaving a friend hanging in general that they stuck out the wait.

As it became apparent that my childhood experience waiting for Razor Ramon might recreate itself, I started collecting consolation prizes. When we were close enough to see the staging area where Hart sat, I lifted my phone over my head, zoomed in as far as possible, and stole blurry photographs of the Hitman. I snagged a sign that must have been posted well before we arrived, back when such a sign would have been necessary, indicating LINE TO MEET BRET HITMAN HART STARTS HERE.

At last, the inevitable happened, when we were within shouting distance, maybe twenty people in front of us, the line was being cut off. Hart had to go, and we weren't going to get to meet him.

My friends eyed me carefully, as if to see if I'd have an outburst of anger or tears or if I'd somehow give them a clear indication it was OK to joke about our bad luck or poor choice not to get to the game earlier.

It was then that I stole the greatest consolation prize of all. For it was then that Hart and his entourage were, at best, ten yards from me and I made a beeline for the Hitman, hopping a haphazardly strung security rope to reach him. Unlike the fan who'd tackle him years later at a WWE Hall of Fame ceremony, I only extended my hand to a few inches from him. He shook it, and I thanked him for being there.

And that might have been enough. I met him. I touched him. I thanked him. And though my treasured copy of his autobiography that got me through the first lonely weeks of an out-of-town move years earlier was left unsigned, and though I had no photograph of the two of us, might that moment have been enough?

Two days later, a Saturday, I went to Hart's website, clicked on the appearances tab.

Another signing. Another minor league baseball game, that very night, a three-hour drive away.

I didn't have any plans.

I fleetingly thought of inviting my friends along. I was certain they wouldn't want to go, and worried one might feel guilty about me making the journey alone and come out of obligation. So, I hit the road solo, only a copy of Truman Capote's *In Cold Blood* that I'd been reading for company. Something to read in the likely case I came upon a long line.

And there was a long line. I stood with my Capote and with Hart's memoir again. Passersby stole looks at the cover of the former, surely curious which wrestler's book it might be, surely mystified at what they saw. I'm not sure if those familiar with Capote would be more impressed with my literary acumen, or wary of the man standing alone in line, reading a murder book.

I'd gotten to this signing earlier this time, relative to the advertised start time, but on a Saturday night, at a stadium I gauged to serve a bigger market, I wound up in a comparable place in line. A pair of teenagers in front of me speculated about if they'd ever get to meet Hart, and I gave them the heads up about my experience from two nights before. Another half hour, despite making decent progress forward, one of them commented that if they hadn't reached Hart in an hour, he was cutting toward the front of the line.

I considered the prospect of failure again, conducting the mental math again as it pertained to the likelihood of ever reaching the front of the line. I decided that, if I didn't at least see it through, it would mean more than the original wasted night, but a three hour drive there, a three hour drive back, a couple hours in line all squandered.

Hadn't my childhood self watched The Hitman stare down steeper odds? Against Yokozuna, more than twice his weight? Against Razor Ramon, bigger, too, by every measure.

I waited.

I waited until the line in front of me had grown much shorter—shorter even than the line two nights before had ever gotten—but after the line behind me had dwindled, too, from what must have been a hundred autograph seekers to not more than a couple dozen weary fans.

I waited until a gray-haired man in a suit came to talk to us. I feared the worst.

But rather than telling us all to go home, he said, "We're going to get everybody through to meet Mr. Hart, but we've gotta be fast. Have your cameras and whatever you want signed ready."

And we moved. There may be some correlation between quantity of time spent on an interaction and the quality of it, but in this case, everyone got their photos and their autographs, right up until it was my turn.

I'd thought about what I might say to Hart. In my more optimistic moments on the drive, I imagined telling him about how he'd helped a scrawny kid believe in himself, or how my best friend and I used to take turns putting the Sharpshooter on each other, or how I'd always favored him over Shawn Michaels, or how I'd watched his matches with Mr. Perfect and Bob Backlund and The 1-2-3 Kid and Steve Austin over and over again.

In an interaction reduced to twenty, maybe thirty seconds—barely longer than the handshake I'd stolen from him two nights before—all I told him was that I was big fan.

But I got my photograph shaking his hand this time. And I got his book signed on the title page, in metallic marker script.

Mission accomplished.

I've met other wrestlers. I got my photo taken with Roddy Piper the first time I went to WrestleMania, in Houston, at an Axxess session designed for long lines. I met Chris Jericho at a book signing for his second memoir, where I told him about being there for his match at that WrestleMania, and he struggled to remember which one I was talking about.

I met Tatanka at an indie wrestling show where he had a table set up, and I actually got to talk to him for the better part of ten minutes for the lack of a line (he told me a lot of people were clamoring for a WrestleMania 9 rematch between him and Shawn Michaels, despite the nearly twenty years that had passed in between). I met Tommy Dreamer, drenched in sweat after an indie match, and only learned later that he never left a fan hanging, after an experience in his own youth when Bob Backlund made him wait for an autograph, only to sneak out a back door. I met Mick Foley, Harley Race, Nick Bockwinkel, Diamond Dallas Page, Sean Waltman, Samoa Joe, Jushin Liger, Marty Jannetty, Mike and Maria Kanellis, The Powers of Pain, The Young Bucks, Manami Toyota, Jerry Lynn, and Christopher Daniels, too.

I don't foresee myself waiting in long lines again, though. Not ones that will leave me standing much more than an hour. Or two.

There are only three professional wrestlers I've called my favorite.

I waited for Razor Ramon.

I got to shake Bret Hart's hand twice. I reckon I earned it each time.

My wife and I attended WrestleMania 33 in Orlando on a belated honeymoon. We spent two days at Universal Studios, concentrated on the Wizarding World of Harry Potter, more out of her obsession than my interest. Then I had my Sunday.

The morning of the PPV, I saw on social media that Hulk Hogan was signing autographs at his new store in Orlando, a clear bid to cash in on hardcore fans in town for WrestleMania. As we waited to be seated at a diner for breakfast, I mapped the distance between the location The Hulkster identified on Twitter and where we stood.

Serendipity called. Google Maps estimated us to be a four-minute walk away.

I didn't rush things. After two days on our feet in amusement park lines, I wanted to enjoy our first proper sit-down meal in days, and indulge in WrestleMania Sunday, which I revered as a holiday second only to Christmas.

But after breakfast, we made our way over. Hogan's people hadn't opened the doors yet. The line of wrestling fans holding vintage action figures, replica championship belts, and old programs wrapped around the building. Sizing it up, based on experience, I guessed that it would take forty-five minutes to wait in this line if I hopped in then; maybe up to an hour and a half if Hogan stopped to chat up every customer.

A woman wandered the line, calling out in a nasally voice to confirm everyone waiting in line had already purchased their tickets.

I asked her how much tickets were.

I don't remember the exact figure that came back. It had to have been more than a hundred dollars. It probably wasn't more than three hundred. Regardless, it was a sum that I could afford, but that nonetheless felt like an awful lot, particularly when I was paying to get in a line after waiting two hours in line the day before to take a rollercoaster ride through Hogwarts. All of this, while Hogan was less than a year removed from his nadir, the scandal of leaked audio that captured him using the n-word pretty liberally.

That, and my wife, who thinks wrestling is fun enough, but has never followed the stories for more than two consecutive weeks–had already submitted to five hours-plus in a stadium full of wrestling fans for later in the day.

She said we could wait if I wanted to.

But I didn't want to.

I wanted to steal a look at Hogan through the glass doors. I did, garnering blurry, sunlight-reflecting-off-smudged-glass photos of him at the autograph table in the process. And that felt like enough.

I'd waited in line to meet wrestlers.

But not that day. We went back to the hotel for a nap and a snack, then on to WrestleMania.

Then on with my life.

MAGGIE DOVE
She Wears The Batman

I've always been a letter writer. I assume this is because talking to people in-person makes me want to kill myself.

There's any number of reasons for these feelings, but the main culprit is probably that for days and days after I interact with anybody, the sound of my own voice replays in my head at 200 mental-decibels while I mercilessly beat myself up for saying whatever incredibly stupid thing I said.

When I get nervous talking to someone, which is most of the time, I lose all ability to control the words that come out of my mouth, and I end up saying something to the effect of, "Sure I like Dave Matthews Band - they're like Phish meets *Sleepless in Seattle*," even though I don't like Dave Matthews Band, I don't like Phish, I have never seen *Sleepless in Seattle*, and the entire string of words makes no sense at all except that Dave Matthews and Tom Hanks have somehow become twins over the years, which is probably the reason my brain made that connection.

As it's coming out of my mouth, I'm thinking, "What the hell are you saying? Jesus! Just shut up!"

It's nothing personal, Dave Matthews Band. I get that you're all talented players and whatnot, but I just generally prefer that a song not start on my 20th birthday and then continue through my 40th. *Wrap it up, guys.* If you can't get it said in a three-minute song, you're just being self-indulgent. A song is a ditty, not a manifesto.

Also, everything I write is a manifesto, so don't even try to get smart with me about my tendency to be long-winded with your "Oh yeah? What about you? What about YOU???"

I come from a large Southern family - being long-winded is a mandate with regard to storytelling, so shut up.

I know you were expecting a "bless your heart" in place of that "shut up," since for some reason people think that all people from the South are genteel while being passive aggressive, but we're not that kind of Southern family. We're more of the variety that will slash your tires with a pocket knife in a Walmart parking lot after we overhear you calling us "too thick to be wearing those stretch pants" in the 10 items or less line. As if you have room to talk in your oversized Tweety Bird t-shirt and elastic-waistband jeans. Get real, Peggy.

As you know, my love of letter writing started in early middle school. Teeny Bopper magazines had whole pages where they listed all the various contact addresses for people like Kirk Cameron, Corey Haim, Giovanni Ribisi, and of course, my favorite, New Kids on The Block. They were just fan club and management addresses and not the actual home addresses of the teen idols, but there were always these nagging, persistent thoughts swimming around in my 12-year-old mind that made me pick up the pen and start writing anyway.

What if your letter is the one Corey Haim actually picks up out of the pile and reads? What if fate somehow intervenes in your otherwise shitty adolescent life, and he walks through the fan club office to sign some paperwork and then right before he leaves, he leans over and picks one envelope out of the pile and it's your letter? You can't win if you don't bet!

As an aside, this would really be an excellent beginning of a gambling addiction story were I a gambling addict - which I'm not. I just happen to get heart palpitations anytime I hear someone yell, "And they're off!" on television.

I also may have cried the first time I won a real bet. And the second time. And the third. And most times. None of the aforementioned facts mean that I have a problem. I'm just a "Gambling Fan". Any time I've looked wild-eyed to the sky, clutched a pile of cash in my hands and yelled, "I CAN'T LOSE!!!!" it was only because, at that moment, it happened to be true. That's just reporting, not gambling.

As another aside (because the previous derailment wouldn't be enough), I shared a room with my older sister Bonnie growing up, and she was one of those tough bad-ass school-skipping girls who chain-smoked as a member of the dance squad and tormented the ever-loving crap out of me every waking moment. In one of my many bids for revenge, every chance I got, I would pull out all the photos of Wil Wheaton from the Teeny Bopper magazines and then hang them up right over her bed so that when she came home from school with all of her teenage delinquent friends, they would think that she totally had the hots for him.

Not that there's anything wrong with Wil Wheaton, far from it. I really like Wil Wheaton. I follow his blog on the internet and he seems like a really solid human being. I was and still am a huge Star Trek fan and The Next Generation is by far my favorite incarnation of the franchise. The thing was, when Bonnie was a teenager, she tended to date either guys in their 20s with mustaches and felony convictions or guys in the military without mustaches who had only joined the military to avoid felony convictions. Wil Wheaton wasn't going to cut it with her bad boy dating reputation. This was early Wesley Crusher-era Wil Wheaton we're talking about here, perhaps the sweetest-looking teenage boy who ever lived.

If I ran out of space on Bonnie's wall to tack up Wil Wheaton photos, I would tack them up to the ceiling over her bed because, like the native peoples of yore with a fresh buffalo kill, I liked to use every part of a Teeny Bopper magazine. By the time I got done going at one with a pair of scissors, they were just shredded bits of nothing and maybe a lone photo of Paula Abdul. I squeezed every penny's worth out of those bastards.

Bonnie would come home, find the Wil Wheaton photos on her wall, tear them off the wall and yell, "STOP PUTTING THESE PICTURES ON MY SIDE OF THE ROOM, ASSHOLE!" and then, most often, drag me out of the room by my hair.

I would do it again with the next month's issues. It didn't matter if I caught a beating over it. It was worth it every single time that I got to watch her jump on the bed and angrily snatch Wil Wheaton pictures off the ceiling in her acid-washed jeans and white half-shirt, eyes rimmed raccoon-like with loads of black eyeliner, while yellow ceiling popcorn rained down on her. It was the best thing that ever happened.

As a matter of fact, she has a 50th birthday coming up in a handful of years, so I'm thinking that maybe I'll break into her house and wallpaper her kitchen with vintage Wil Wheaton photos as a surprise. Maybe I'll start a fundraiser and beg and plead and eventually pay for Wil Wheaton to make a personal appearance as she blows out the candles. Plus, I think we're finally at an age where if she started some shit over it, I could totally take her.

That is the biggest lie anyone has ever told.

Bonnie's the kind of person who will still be able to beat the crap out of anybody even if she's 80, because that girl fights <u>dirty</u>. Anyone who knows her is nodding their head right now and saying, "Oh, that bitch'll mess you UP."

So back to the magazine pages with all the contact addresses, which started, like, thirty paragraphs ago.

With every Teeny Bopper magazine I bought, I would sit with pen in-hand and circle the addresses of which teen idols I was going to write to that month. I would take my marked-up list and get out my best south-western print stationery in either turquoise or peach, carefully write out my fan letters over the course of a Saturday afternoon, and then unfurl the roll of postage stamps that I had "liberated" from one of the doctors' offices I cleaned at night, affix the postage, and drop the letters into the outgoing mail on Monday.

It was totally worth all the work of letter writing, too, because with only one exception, the teen idol's contact people would actually send you something back. It was usually a form letter thanking you for your support, but with an ink signature that you were supposed to believe was actually penned by the teen idol himself. If you sent in a self-addressed stamped envelope, they might even send you a packet of stickers or an iron-on for a t-shirt.

I remember the first response I ever got. It was from Corey Haim. I held the autographed form response letter up to the light and determined that it had definitely been signed by an actual human being; therefore, there was no reason to believe that Corey Haim hadn't been the one who had actually signed it. It had to be his real signature, or else it would have been silly for me to have then slept with the letter under my pillow for the next ~~two years~~ month. That's MONTH. <u>One</u> month.

John Stamos sent back a black and white photo postcard with a stamped autograph on it. Tina Ferrari, my and everyone else's favorite lady wrestler from G.L.O.W., sent back an autographed color picture, and Chad Allen sent back an 8" x 10" black and white glossy picture that had "Reach for the stars!" written on it with his autograph underneath. A simple smear test determined this was machine-printed onto the photo, but it looked real enough that when I stuck it into a picture frame with glass over it, you couldn't tell.

I don't know what Giovanni Ribisi typically sent back because I never wrote to him. Like most Gen-X women, I didn't find him attractive until he got much older and adopted that shifty, homeless, French drug dealer look he's been rolling with the past twenty years. This is because I, like most Gen-X women, was manipulated by movies and television into thinking that a guy sporting a shifty, homeless, French drug dealer aesthetic is secretly just a damaged genius who you can fix with the right combination of love, devotion, methadone, and flea shampoo.

The one teen idol who never wrote me back, despite my sending him approximately twenty letters over a two-year period, was Jordan Knight from New Kids on The Block.

Naturally, I surmised that this was because he was in love with me and he was just too afraid to tell me.

If watching a hundred hours of 80s sitcoms a week had taught me anything, it was that boys were terrified to tell girls about their feelings and could only reveal their crushes on you by hiring Menudo to play at your birthday party. This is a rookie mistake, by the way, because as I've said before and will say a thousand times more if that's what I have to do to make the world understand: **If you invite Menudo to your girl's party, your girl is leaving with Menudo.**

It's like inviting a pile of strippers to your husband's birthday party thinking that he'll be really excited to have sex with *you* after they leave. Get some sense.

Why didn't Jordan Knight respond to my many letters? I don't know; it's a question I ask myself every day. Perhaps I had come on too strong with my first letter, where I told him how "fine" I thought he was, and how he was by far the best dancer in the group, and that he and I were destined to be together forever and ever and if he just met me in person he would look into my eyes and see it, too. I also mentioned that he had the most enviable rat-tail in the group. The way it bounced off his back as he ran in slow motion in the video for "Please Don't Go Girl"...

... I'm quivering.

Since I didn't get a response with my first letter, I decided to take a few different approaches with each subsequent letter. Sometimes I would take a casual, conversational tone where I pretended we already knew each other. I would tell him about what I did the previous weekend, what other music I was listening to, how much the seventh grade totally sucked. Sometimes I would try to appeal to his visually-driven male brain and send a photo of myself in my new jean shorts that I got from J. Byrons for my birthday.

One time I tried to pique his interest with a bribe in the form of a Burger King coupon for a Buy-One-Get-One-Free Original Chicken Sandwich. I told him that we should get together sometime and share a couple of them. I reminded him that the Original Chicken Sandwich was by far my favorite in the Burger King line-up, if not in all fast food line-ups, so that he would fully understand the kind of sacrifice I was making by offering to share my coupon with him.

My sister Bonnie worked at Burger King, so it wasn't actually a sacrifice at all given how much free Burger King I got because of the family hook-up, but Jordan Knight didn't need to be privy to that knowledge. As far as he knew, this was the last Original Chicken Sandwich coupon in the world.

Still no luck.

My relationship with Jordan Knight started as a one-way flirtation, rolled into an obsession, morphed into an investigation, and eventually devolved into a replication. I "Single White Femaled" him years before that was even a thing.

My friend Jenny had the New Kids on The Block "Hangin' Tough" VHS tape, and we would sit and watch it over and over for hours at her house. I tried to replicate every outfit Jordan Knight wore throughout the video in my own wardrobe, which mostly meant that I owned every Batman logo t-shirt in town. I begged my mother to let me dye my platinum-blonde hair jet-black so that I could look more like him. That was a no-go because she apparently HATED ME AND NEVER WANTED ME TO FIND LOVE. At least that's what I told myself at the time. (In truth, that woman adores me.)

What teen idol didn't want to date a 12-year-old girl who looked exactly like him? I was pretty sure that if Jordan Knight and I ever ended up in the same room together, he would spot my Batman logo t-shirt from across the room, look down at his own Batman logo t-shirt, and make the connection:

"She wears The Batman."

"I wear The Batman."

"I marry the girl."

The irony of this line of thinking, of course, is that musicians really are all so enamored of themselves that they essentially *do* just want to date themselves, so my instincts weren't really that far off. It was just in the execution that I missed the mark.

A Batman logo t-shirt would have worked, had it been on a hot 18-year-old chick as a half-shirt with her lady-mangos hanging out from underneath, along with a pair of hot pants and spiky ankle boots, but per-haps *not* when paired with the combination I had put together. I preferred to wear my Batman logo t-Shirt tucked into my mint green JIMMY'Z surfer shorts with the Velcro faux-belt and round out the ensemble with my gigantic white high-tops. I wouldn't start dressing like jailbait for another year, so I was still a social leper tomboy. I didn't feel that I needed to dress like jailbait at that point because I wasn't really "on the market." After all, I was saving myself for Jordan Knight.

As I got dressed for the New Kids on The Block concert the following year, in my Batman logo t-shirt, I told Mom about my plans, where Jordan Knight was going to spot me in the crowd, send a roadie out to fetch me, then marry me and take me on tour with them.

She said, "Don't hold your breath, kid. I'm sure he has thousands of groupies he boinks regularly."

I protested, "But he's Catholic!"

She responded by saying, "Are you kidding me? They're the worst ones!"

I reminded myself that she was totally biased because she HATED ME AND NEVER WANTED ME TO FIND LOVE.

Throughout the concert, I was certain Jordan Knight was making eye contact with me, despite the fact that my seat was approximately 10,000 yards from the stage and there were 40,000 other screaming girls there. After the show, I waited outside the arena, along with around 5,000 of my closest fellow fans for their motorcade to pass. I expected the limo door to open, Jordan Knight's arm to shoot out from behind the door frame, and then snatch me up and pull me inside. Then he would marry me.

Instead, a police motorcade escorted Donny Wahlberg, whom I considered to be clearly a lesser New Kid, out through the crowd on a motorcycle. He was wearing overalls with no shirt underneath, and something like "Crack is Wack!" was airbrushed across the denim pocket on the front. Jordan Knight was nowhere in sight. My heart sank as Donnie Wahlberg rode off into the Crack is Wack sunset.

That was the day I almost became a cynic about letter writing. But, despite having my heart shredded like so many unwanted Wil Wheaton posters above my sister's bed, I continued writing letters to teen idols, and as I grew up and moved into high school and my musical taste changed, I wrote to hair bands and grunge bands and post-grunge bands.

The last letter I wrote was actually to my beloved, most favorite band in the whole world, Superdrag. It was 1996 and I was 20, way past the age where people still wrote to bands, and I wrote to tell them how much I loved them when I saw them play two shows that summer, and I thanked them for showing me and my best friend Anne such a good time on their tour bus afterwards (uh huh). Over the years, bands didn't really have the teen idol machinery to write back or send form letter responses, so I wasn't expecting anything back.

I neglected to mention to them in my letter that I slept with their debut CD under my pillow. I was 20 years old now, and after you pass, oh, say age 14 or so, that's no longer a testament to your fandom. Sleeping with someone's CD under your pillow when you're 20 is a testament to your "problems." I hoped they had remembered me because the singer, John Davis, had complimented my cool pants on both nights that we hung out with the band, so I signed the letter "Maggie Dove - Queen of Cool Pants."

It was quite a surprise a month later to pull an envelope out of the mailbox that was addressed to: *Maggie Dove "Queen of Cool Pants."*

So! In summary: You can't win if you don't bet.

If you invite Menudo to your girl's party, your girl is leaving with Menudo.

JACOB FOWLER
An Elegy for the King of Parodies

Bart Baker's YouTube channel is dormant. According to his Twitter account, the only way to listen to his new content is by changing your phone settings so that you can access the Chinese version of the App Store. Which is to say, Bart has dropped out of American pop culture. But he had a substantial career on YouTube, one that I was obsessed with; an obsession fueled not by enjoyment but by hatred and repugnance.

Bart Baker is a content creator on YouTube specializing in song parodies of pop music. He has been posting on YouTube since 2006 and has been a partner with the site since 2009. He currently has over ten million subscribers and has amassed over three billion views (this can be found on his IMDB and SocialBlade page). At one point he dubbed himself "The King of Parodies." It is nugatory as to how well that title stuck, but his view counts relative to his contemporary parodists seems to support this bold claim. His wide audience and self-insertion into mainstream popular culture makes him, to me, a figure in contemporary pop culture. However, he has not posted since September of 2018 and, as aforementioned, seems to have shifted away from his original parody-making endeavor in favor of becoming an international rapper and pop singer. His new persona is "Lil Kloroxx" and it seems to be Bart's iteration of the popular "SoundCloud rapper" genre. But I was never obsessed with Lil Kloroxx; I was obsessed with Bart.

Bart captured my attention when I was in college. One of his videos found its way into my recommended section due to YouTube's convoluted recommendation algorithm. I watched the video, and then another, and then five more. I showed my roommate and he too immediately became obsessed. We latched onto him like a Remora fish on a shark; he was an unstoppable force of grotesque absurdity and we could not get enough. I don't think I have ever laughed at a Bart Baker video. His content is not enticing because it is comedically sound or has any type of artistic merit, rather it is enticing because it is great content to "hate watch." My roommate and I spent plenty of late nights cringing, yelling at our TV, and being repulsed as we watched Bart's content. There are many reasons to dislike Bart's content, but let us distill it down to two main points: Bart's content is predatory, and it is malicious.

First, Bart preys on people in several ways. The most egregious way is that even though his productions are funded by large production studios, he still advertises and extorts his mainly juvenile audience. YouTube demographics are easy to access and successful creators like Bart know exactly what groups are watching their videos. His main demographic is children. Most of Bart's videos end with a two to three-minute-long plea to his viewers imploring that they buy his branded merchandise or download an app or click on some link so that he can earn money. He even once made a video (that was not a parody) where he sat in front of a camera and basically took his viewers hostage suggesting that if he doesn't get more money soon, he would stop making videos. I am more than willing to acknowledge that capitalism forces artists into monetizing their art in ways that will make them uncomfortable. This is a systemic issue that all creators deal with. However, it is possible for Bart to advertise and support himself with his creation (especially since he has funding from lager studios) without demanding that children donate to him or download sketchy extensions on their parents' browsers.

Secondly, his content is malicious. It is not my desire is not to relish in Bart's maliciousness, but readers unfamiliar with his work need to understand the essence of what he does. Thus, let us sprint through a quick recapitulation of five of Bart's parodies. He has a parody with a twist at the end where Bart reveals that the rapper Silento is actually Jared Fogle in an elaborate disguise. Another parody has seven uninterrupted seconds of close-ups of actors' butts, accompanied by fart noises. He has a parody featuring domestic abuse jokes at the expense of Rihanna. He has another parody wherein Ariana Grande is portrayed as being in the middle of a literal tug-of-war between Bill Cosby and Donald Trump, one of whom is trying to deport her and the other is trying to sexually harass her; this parody concludes with Bart, who is portraying Caitlyn Jenner, running over the trio with a car. Finally, Bart has a parody where he plays Meghan Trainor and is turned into shrimp tempura at the end.

These parodies each have twenty-one, thirty, twenty-seven, twenty-two, and sixteen million views respectively. They all contain some level of bigotry, misogyny, or bad faith attacks. They are not aberrations, rather endemic of Bart's style and flavor. They are offensive, cringey, and have never made me laugh. I have reported all of them.

However, they all have an overwhelmingly positive like-to-dislike ratio, and based on the comments, his viewers seem extremely supportive of his content. But perhaps the most surprising aspect is that I cannot find any negative reactions to him. A "Bart Baker sucks" Google search reveals no relevant results, and I have yet to see any popular YouTube reaction channels respond to any of his patently heinous videos.

Bart's channel is filled with nothing but hatred. It is an amalgamation of bigotry, misogyny, racism, and a manifest lack of humor. Why did I obsess over it? Why is it so well received? I think it is because there is something compelling about watching demolition. And that is what his videos are: demolition. Demolition of the structure of parody, demolition of any expectations of good faith, demolition of respect, of kindness.

While Bart's channel seems like an anomaly, it is not. This type of obscene entertainment is not a divergence from popular culture but rather a major component of it.

There is something enticing about watching demolition. I am hesitant to call it "enjoyment," but it is certainly consuming. This obsession with demolition predates my relationship with Bart Baker or anyone's obsession with any pop culture figure. This obsession seems inherent to human nature. It is why CNN continually played Trump rallies and press conferences during the 2016 election, it is why people gravitate to shows with gratuitous violence and YouTube videos containing violence that TV cannot, it is why gladiator fights were so popular in the Roman Empire.

What we have in common with all other dabblers in pop culture and with our Ancient Roman predecessors is a desire to *observe* but not *partake*. We think to ourselves, "I'll just watch. I won't actually do that." But in our role as observer, the most active participation we can take is simply *watching*. By watching, we are supporting. Either we give our money directly to a ticket taker, or we give ad revenue, or we give a massive platform to an outsider candidate and end up with a game show host president. Thus, our decisions to interact with malicious and overly offensive pop culture has negative impacts in the material world. A choice to passively observe is in many ways a choice to support. At the very least this decision to watch legitimizes the content. For four years I inadvertently gave credence to Bart's atrocious content. I watched ironically, with hate in my heart, but I still watched.

Our actions, our choices regarding entertainment, have tangible effects and consequences that we must be ready to account for. This conclusion is rather anodyne. Of course our actions have consequences, this is something we've been told since we were children. But entertainment, pop culture, is supposed to be an escape from those responsibilities. It is not. Instead we must live with our entertainment choices perhaps not as a moral indictment but as an exercise in morality. We must remain conscious of the effects of what we choose to watch. These decisions are not removed from our larger sense of morality but are contingent on it. But, since the question of morality is far too large for the scope of this essay, it might be better to say: choose obsessions wisely.

I say this not from a place of authority or probity, but rather from below the reader. I made the worst possible choice for four years! I watched content that only drew me in because of how awful I knew it would be. I wanted to hate watch it. And even if I did not agree with a single bigoted stance or laugh at a single offensive joke, I still watched it. I still gave Bart ad revenue by clicking, more views by clicking, a larger platform by clicking. My collegiate years were spent obsessing over these gross misrepresentations of pop culture. I was consumed by Bart Baker's awfulness. My entertainment choices mirrored the violence and horror I saw happening in the material world around me. I was fueled by shame and hate, a rather inappropriate combination for informing consumer choices.

Bart Baker's channel is dead: good. My obsession can die and hopefully turn into something else. Yet my yearning for demolition will, unfortunately, not evaporate with Bart's pop culture relevance, it will instead look for something else to latch on to. However, my desire for demolition, just like everyone's, requires vigilance. I hope that I learn from my time with Bart and make better choices.

MADELINE LANE-MCKINLEY
A Love Letter to Pee-Wee

Sometime last year a question occurred to me. It was the seed of a speculative fiction.

I began to wonder about an alternate history in which Paul Reubens did not go to visit his relatives in Sarasota, Florida in July of 1991. Reubens didn't visit Florida, and on July 26th, he didn't go to an adult movie theater where he and three other men were arrested during a routine undercover police operation. This would be a world in which, though it had already ended after a sixth season, *Pee-Wee's Playhouse* went into syndication on CBS. This is a world in which I would've been able to keep watching and loving Pee-Wee.

Pee-Wee Herman was my first crush. This has nothing to do with Reubens. When I was six years old, my life goal wasn't really to be Pee-Wee's lover or "wife," but to be something like Pee-Wee's permanent housemate, just like Chairy and Pterri and Genie. I didn't really know who Reubens was, or maybe I didn't care. Who I knew, or thought I knew, was Pee-Wee.

Pee-Wee was always laughing, never not at play. He lived for experiments, jokes, and friendships. I'm not sure how Pee-Wee supported himself, but then again, he lived in a world without money. Jobs existed in *Pee-Wee's Playhouse* only for the purpose of play and care. It was a world firmly against adulthood.

Almost as soon as I discovered Pee-Wee, he was taken away from me.

*

At first, I didn't know why. The show, I remember thinking, wasn't "good for children." I picked that up somewhere – maybe from Peter Jennings, or from some conversation adults were having in the other room.

When the idea of this alternate history came to me, I was thinking a lot about something that had happened to me a few years later in my chronology, which is where I started to learn about these speculative exercises.

The question I repeated for a long time was, "What if that hadn't happened? Who would I be?" And occasionally it's quite strange to see how the question of "Who would I be?" somehow means "Where would I be?"

The truth is that I don't remember when I learned what actually happened with Reubens in the adult theater. By the time I was a teenager, I began to understand that period as a battleground for "family values" launched by the right; but back when I was six, it was such a mystery. I'm not sure how I made sense of why Pee-Wee disappeared, or why he left so suddenly.

A few weeks ago, I started reading about what happened in the weeks after Reubens's arrest. Celebrities came to his defense -- like Cyndi Lauper, who wrote "She-Bop!" and understood the "family values" attack so intimately.

And then there was Bill Cosby. When Cosby was on her show, Oprah asked him what parents should tell their kids about Pee-Wee. His answer, we know by now, had nothing to do with Pee-Wee. And oddly, he kept referring to Reubens as "Mr. Hermann":

> "...when he wasn't there, off stage, he did this, or what-ever. And then, look at only that part. Look at only the part where he's teaching. And whatever else happens over here ... it's too deep to go into because so many answers come about. But I just feel that everyone should, we should all look and see if there's some way that things could be redeemable."

The joke is obvious, but there is something else there. The family values Cosby then stood for remains the mechanism of the kind of abuse he is now a figure of.

Of course, that's obvious, too: fathers get to be abusers – not queer weirdos with "playhouses."

Like so many kids, I was raised to worry about strangers. But I wasn't constantly monitored – I just worried a lot. I'm still afraid of vans. Pee-Wee was the first version of the "stranger," but I soon learned – perhaps before discovering the details of his arrest – that it was his sexuality that made him dangerous, and I began to assume he was gay. Back then "gay" was the word we would use for it. Now I'd say "queer."

What was most queer about Pee-Wee was his relationship toward his own adulthood. He rejected adulthood, including the obligation toward a sexual identity. He was "gay" in the sense that I loved that he was "gay," whatever that meant – it wasn't a problem for me. For me, the appeal was mostly just about being his housemate – and possibly, much more strongly, getting out of my own household.

Just as Cosby was in a position to redeem Reubens, it was the man who molested me who most explicitly condemned Pee-Wee (not Reubens) in my memory from that time. It's strange to me that I remembered that so vividly – his homophobic tirades against Pee-Wee, which stuck with me for years before I would realize that strangers were the least of my worries.

*

Recently I described myself as a "fag hag" and realized that that was, actually, my first sexual identity. I wanted to be proximate to masculine desire, but not the object of it – or the target of it. Pee-Wee, it seems, was my first glimpse of this, however sad and fleeting.

It's a strange thought -- how much we were all parented by network television, for so long.

In the nineties there were lots of fag hags. It's not that they were new. But *Will & Grace* announced this, far more than it announced some version of gay coupledom. It specified elements of this other queer relationship more quickly, or the homosocial relationship that was nevertheless not sexual.

Then it seemed like fag hags were a kind of approximation, though. I never quite had the language for it then. It was a not-quite-coupledom -- something less than, or something not quite. The fag hag appeared so often as a threat, a contaminant or vulnerability. The hag was the straight world, not the ultimate queer. It has taken me time to recover hagdom from this muck – to insist on this as a figure of uncoupling, of libidinal friendship, of non-reproduction, of care. Rather than a failed enactment of heterosexual romance or partial articulation of family life, this dynamic so often takes the shape of a radical refusal that goes unnoticed.

It felt safe but not because it wasn't dangerous. It was always so dangerous.

The summer of 1998, I had become a fag hag for the first time, unless Pee-Wee counts. My friend Chris and I had been inseparable for a brief period that seemed longer then. We watched the same TV shows and liked reading books. He wanted to be a writer before me, but that's because I wanted to be a filmmaker. Because we were always together, and because so many teenagers around us didn't seem to care for *Star Trek: The Next Generation* or whatever else we obsessed over, everyone assumed that we were a couple. And of course, we were a couple. But we weren't the kind they thought.

There were silences between us. I had been wondering a lot about whether I was actually in love with Sinead O'Connor. Chris knew things about me, though he didn't really say them.

There was a day at the end of the summer when Chris called me on the phone with a different tone of voice. There was something weird about how he asked me to do what we would sometimes do in an ordinary way. We met at the mall. I don't remember what I thought he was going to do when we met up. I just remember thinking that something important was about to happen. At first, we took a familiar walk through the mall. There's something so striking about how teenagers occupy shopping malls, or perhaps just used to. We would walk around, sometimes buying a large pretzel or a milkshake, sometimes just a gumball from a machine, but mostly we would take up space there. We sat on the benches, tried on the clothes, smelled the perfume, made fun of fashion trends. That day, we ended up in SEARS. We tried out some chairs and couches, and then laid on a mattress in the bedroom furniture section. I don't remember how Chris told me he was gay, but I remember how we were laying on that mattress, feet apart from each other. Maybe I already actually knew. It didn't change the fact that part of me probably still expected something else to happen: for us to give in to the narrative, to call ourselves a "couple," to take the weird social pressure off of us. Instead, I left that day understanding that I had a secret.

Then about two months later, in October of '98, Matthew Shepard was murdered.

That was the year of the Unabomber and Monica Lewinsky. Kosovo was happening in the background and *Titanic* was all the teenage girls around me wanted to talk about.

What I remember so distinctly was the story of how Matthew Shepard was found. Bludgeoned and tied to a fence, he was first mistaken for a scarecrow. The only parts of his face that weren't covered in blood had been cleaned by streaks of tears.

After Matthew Shepard, keeping Chris's secret felt like an even greater obligation. To play the part of his girlfriend became a form of protection. But the next year, he came out to his family, began dating boys he met on AOL chat rooms, and started frequenting the shitty diner where the closeted boys would learn to tolerate black coffee for the prospect of meeting each other. I began to lose importance in his life, as his life felt more safe, even though it was just that he had learned to become more brave.

Part of being a hag, too, is learning to be left behind.

*

I kept loving Pee-Wee. But I wonder what would have happened. What if Reubens hadn't been arrested. What could childhood have been. What if Pee-Wee had just been in syndication…

These are the type of thoughts that have a way of stacking up.

CHARLES AUSTIN MUIR
Lost in a Debbie Gibson Music Video

Good morning, everyone. I'm Charles Austin Muir. I recognize some of you from my class on Jean-Claude Van Damme. Come to think of it, can anyone name the movie this is from? "How does it feel to be hunted?" Very good, Sophelia, it's from *Hard Target*. Anyway, I appreciate you guys' evals and guess what? I'll be teaching my advanced course, Semiotics and the Asian Fight Spectator in *Bloodsport*, in the spring.

But enough about JCVD.

How many of you have heard of Debbie Gibson?

You're right, Mackayden… our class subject did star in *Mega Shark versus Mecha Shark*. But before that she starred in numerous theatrical productions and even sang on Broadway. She's a real deal musical prodigy. At age 17, Debbie Gibson became the youngest female recording artist to write, produce and perform a Billboard number-one single ("Foolish Beat"). And consider this: She clawed her way to stardom long before the Internet became a thing.

You see, back in the Eighties, an aspiring musical entertainer couldn't become a sensation by simply uploading their video recordings to YouTube. Debbie Gibson spent years knocking on doors and building her repertoire before she scored a contract with Atlantic Records. She even went on tour to push her first hit single, "Only in My Dreams," while attending high school as an honor student. By comparison, I barely graduated with my grueling extracurricular regimen of eating Cheetos and watching *Family Ties* in my bedroom. But I digress.

That's the downside teaching some of these pop culture classes, you know? They make history feel so *personal*.

Let's look at the course syllabus.

"Semiotics and the Music Videos of Debbie Gibson is a critical theory course designed to give students the tools to analyze the entertainer's music videos as patterns of signs that construct a romantic utopia with Gibson playing the star, narrator and instigator." That's a mouthful, isn't it? Simply put, we'll examine how the medium constructs Gibson as a multitalented young artist who articulates the passions of a generation... my generation. We will base our approach on Heidi Peeters's "The Semiotics of Music Videos: It Must be Written in the Stars," which you will find at the link provided in the syllabus.

What's that, Ephemera? What do I mean by "romantic utopia?"

Well, Peeters argues that the music video employs a range of filmic devices to create an ideal world similar to what happens in a musical when a character breaks into song. Only unlike the musical, the music video tends to treat the sequence not as a momentary flight from the narrative, but *as central to the video's ontological basis*. In most music videos, the song and dance act occurs with no outside world waiting for the performer to return to the narrative. This is what I mean by utopia—the absence of any need for the performer to participate in a semblance of normative reality. Instead, the pop artist becomes the star at the center of a utopian universe. In Debbie Gibson's case, a *romantic* utopian universe.

You know what? I haven't given you guys full disclosure.

I have a crush on Gibson. I know how that sounds considering my age, but it's purely nostalgic. I watch her early videos and can't help but think, "Wow, she sure looks like my wife did back then." Kara and I started dating way back in 1989—the year *Electric Youth* came out. Funny how I missed the resemblance for so long. Anyway, about a year ago I came upon the video for "We Could be Together" and realized how much Debbie Gibson reminded me of the girl I later married. They looked alike, dressed alike, danced alike... though my wife insists she had smoother moves than the ones in the video. Unconsciously, I had snagged myself an alternative Debbie Gibson!

Way to go, Professor Muir. Haha.

Sorry, I had to get that off my chest. Like I said, that's the downside teaching pop culture classes. I mean, for example, 1977 is a time marker, right? But if you say, "Bruce Jenner was on a Wheaties box in 1977," suddenly I'm six years old again, chugging milk by the fridge and staring at Bruce Jenner on a Wheaties box when he was Bruce Jenner. I'm just warning you guys these digressions are going to happen the more we dive into Debbie Gibson's music videos.

In fact, let's skip this talk and watch the video for Debbie Gibson's chart-topping ballad, "Lost in Your Eyes."

Okay, we're three minutes in. Pause.

So, here's a good example of the Gibsonian utopia. We see a jump cut from a lip-syncing Gibson to a medium shot of her sweetheart playing a pick-up game in an outdoor basketball court. Cut to Gibson in a different outfit watching from behind a chain-link fence. Seeing her, the boyfriend stops in mid-lay-up and scoops the ball to a player who may or may not be his teammate. The play goes back to the top of the key while he stands there smiling at her. Another jump cut to Gibson lip-syncing in another outfit. Cut to the court again. The couple now has the key to themselves. Gibson fakes the boyfriend out by pointing at the chain-link fence as if she's still standing behind it. She drives past him and puts up a jump shot. He defends by hooking his arm around her waist—why not? It's a win-win for him. Gibson's shot banks in off the backboard, and on a level not visualized in wholesome teen-pop '80s music videos, both players score.

But notice the hoop as a utopian index of the young man's shifting priorities. When we see him driving toward the basket, the scene goes back to Gibson before we see the basket. And when the camera shows Gibson's bank shot, we are shown a hoop without a net. It's as if the game of basketball is losing substance in the video universe. Now earlier, we see the pair watching an outdoor chamber music event. This serves as a syntagmatic link to the parallel edits of Gibson singing and playing piano throughout the video. In Debbie Gibson's musically centered utopia, culture reigns supreme. Which is not to say recreational sports are excluded... as long as the pop star is the one opponent on the basketball court.

I'm afraid I have to digress again, class. Your young, collective presence has helped me realize something. I'm looking at Gibson and her boyfriend paused on the projection screen and seeing the roots of my marriage in a whole new light.

You see, I didn't have a girlfriend through almost all of high school. I went to a predominantly white, private school. I was shy and fell outside the standards of male beauty in that environment. With my brown skin and dark, thick hair, I looked more like an underage fight spectator in *Bloodsport*. Even so, I had a crush on this one girl—Heather Duncan. Secretly, I wanted Heather and I to create something like a Debbie Gibson music video. I would have loved it if we'd run on a beach or snuggled on a carousel while a man wearing shades played a saxophone solo in an abandoned building (which happens in Gibson's video for "Only in My

Dreams"). For four years, I devised many such poetic linkages around my utopian conception of Heather Duncan.

Unfortunately, Heather didn't see me in the same light. The closest I got to her was when she let me carry her books to her bus stop. Things were going all right until we reached the stop where a bunch of our classmates stood on the corner. Heather grabbed her books and ducked into the crowd as if she didn't want to be seen with me. This was 1987 on Valentine's Day. Anyway, when I finally found a girl who liked me, I seized every opportunity to make up for lost romantic montages.

I begged Kara—my wife, now—to go out in my varsity letterman jacket. I played one-on-one with her on the basketball court. I took her to candlelight dinners (although she insisted on going Dutch). On the surface, these or similar acts might be expected of a male suitor in many times and places. But that doesn't speak to the phenomenon of the music video utopia infiltrating my inner world and what is more interesting, *my memory* of that infiltration.

When I started dating Kara, I saw myself as the leading man in our own music video. And together we produced a string of rituals that at least approximated the effect of a music video utopia. We did not live in that realm obviously, but we appreciated (or at least I did) when our sensory inputs corresponded to the actions and settings in a music video. With age, however, I can get a little closer to perfection.

I'm forty-seven now. People my age were the first kids to let musical entertainers whisk them into tightly constructed television wonderlands full of sentimental montages and dreamy imagery on a daily basis. As a result of their imprint, my memory edits certain episodes in my life in the style of the videos I watched when both the medium and I were young. Sure, this involves cognitive bias. But my version of simplifying and exaggerating memories is not only a matter of psychology. It's a matter of technology—the cable television technology that transmitted MTV utopias into my brain.

Now I don't just judge the past more favorably than the present. I assemble it into visual sequences that evoke an emotional response I have only ever had to music videos. In my mind's eye I see slow dissolves of Kara and I walking in the park, kissing under a tree, drinking Dairy Queen milk shakes, all of it imbued with the spirit of getting-to-know-each-other and eternal youth. In a nutshell, I'm finally getting the *feeling* I tried to capture in those early years… the bliss of a courtship detached from the mundane world.

What's that? Well, of course, Bracksleigh, I know I'm romanticizing the past. It's *how* I romanticize it—the utopian video-inspired mechanism— that's what I thought you guys would find interesting.

Remember what I said about Bruce Jenner on a Wheaties box? If you say, "Mark Goodman used to host *MTV US Top 20 Countdown*," I'm right back in my dad's rocking chair watching the veejay introduce Simple Minds's "Don't You (Forget about Me)" when I should be doing homework. So, when my memories play back as montages, I'm actually receiving two sets of feelings: Those aroused by the music video-like presentation and those arising from my earliest relationship to music videos. Keep in mind I was a kid when MTV first went on the air. I didn't have to make a living and my hip didn't hurt.

Listen, I'm going to let you guys in on something. I'm not too pleased with life right now. The mundane world has really been sticking it to me. You want to know the worst of it? My wife is ill. Like, seriously ill. We're talking *The Amityville Horror*-in-your-insides ill. Ghosts of old traumas dragging her down to the basement and showing her the passage to Hell. That's simplifying the matter, but even so it feels like a horror movie when I see my closest friend of thirty years struggle to keep the light in her eyes. I believe Kara can go into remission, but I hate being powerless to do anything but assist with the day-to-day. Get groceries, feed the dogs, load the dishwasher, all the boring stuff I didn't help her out enough with before.

And with all this going on, the universe isn't giving us any breaks. Did I mention that last month two different drivers hit our car and our sewer backed up and flooded the basement? Yeah, you know what? Fuck the universe.

Guys, I want to try something. Channel your collective energy into the frozen image on the projection screen. Help me get inside the image. Pretend this is a *Twilight Zone* episode about a middle-aged professor who desperately wants to escape into a Debbie Gibson music video. What I have in mind isn't as creepy as it sounds.

Keep channeling, guys. Whoa, did anyone see the projection screen shimmer just now like a wavy dream sequence effect? Holy crap... this might work.

Let's try a mantra to blow the mystical portal wide open.

"I was seventeen years old when 'Lost in Your Eyes' came out."

Go ahead, class, say it.

"I was seventeen years old when 'Lost in Your Eyes' came out."

Again.

"I was seventeen years old when 'Lost in Your Eyes' came out."

Again.

"I was seventeen years old when 'Lost in Your Eyes came out."

Louder.

"I was seventeen years old when 'Lost in Your Eyes' came out."

I can't hear you!

"I was seventeen years old when 'Lost in Your Eyes' came out."

Wow, I think it's

say it

lost

I was

seventeen years

lost

working

lost in

    LOST IN

      LOST IN

        LOST IN

          LOST IN

I'm

falling

this is

hold on

ayyyyyyyyyyy

Whoa.

Guys… I think we did it. I can't see a thing. But it's like a fog bank is breaking up. Not really, but sort of. This must be a fade-in to an establishing shot. Wait. I'm seeing trees… a stone bridge… leaves on the ground… a cement path. I'm in a park. I'm wearing my British Knights and my varsity letterman jacket. Let's see—my hairline is lower and my jeans are tighter. Oh my God, I'm seventeen again!

Okay, I'm taking the cement path up a hill. Man, it smells nice. Like a group of volleyball players racing by me on their way to practice. This is amazing. Thank you for transporting me here, kids, thank you! Jeez… I feel kind of bad, but I have to get one more thing off my chest before I reach the top of the hill and leave you all in my dust.

Um… you're not real, guys. You're a device I thought up to help make me the star of this essay. You're the rhetorical equivalent of, say, a frame story in a music video. You gave me a framework to examine my nostalgic obsession with Debbie Gibson as well as an opportunity to make fun of Gen Z names and academics who use adjectives like "Gibsonian." I'm sorry.

But that doesn't mean this is a work of fiction. Everything else is based on fact. Debbie Gibson really did become the youngest female recording artist to write, produce and perform a number-one single. Charles Austin

Muir really did spend his high school years eating Cheetos and watching *Family Ties* in his bedroom and fantasizing about a girl named Heather Duncan (although her name wasn't Heather Duncan). And he really did start dating his future wife the year *Electric Youth* topped the Billboard 200. And his wife really is struggling with an illness and he really believes she can go into remission. And he knows writing about himself in third person and starting a bunch of sentences with "And" can seem pompous. But it feels so good right now. Anyway, I'm sorry, you guys. I let you down. But hey, you see where it got me? I'm in a freaking music video.

I'm almost to the top of the hill now. The path is leading me right where I want to go.

Look, I know I can't stay in this place for long. I also know the Eighties was not a better time than any other. I also know '80s music videos were predominantly white—meaning I didn't see much of myself represented in them—just like my high school. This is *my* '80s music video though, so I get to be the leading man here. I won't feel like a fight-crowd extra in a Jean-Claude Van Damme movie.

I'm at the top of the hill now, guys. My God, my girlfriend looks radiant. She's in a blue and white crop top that looks shoulder-padded (but isn't) and rolled-up jean shorts. She has the court to herself. She's at the top of the key. She's bouncing the ball. She notices me. I line up on defense. She points at the chain-link fence. I go for her fake and when she slips past me, I pull her back and hold her tight.

She flings the ball in a high arc.

We both score.

Update: Kara Muir was diagnosed with stage 4 colorectal cancer 41 days after I submitted this story. We thought she had inflammatory bowel disease, an opinion backed initially by her physician. She is going through both Western and holistic treatments. We still have hope for a remission. As she says, "Your story isn't over until you are."

MARK A. NOBLES
Tom Cruise Can Kiss My Ass

I was a rebel in my youth. I was my own man. In 1977 I was the guy with the 'Disco Sucks' bumper sticker on my 1969 Triumph Spitfire. In 1982 I confidently stated to my English professor that Hemingway was a hack, and Shakespeare was an overrated plagiarist. I cut my own path through early adulthood, or so I told myself.

In the Spitfire I listened to cassette tapes because I was in control of the music I listened to and besides, Top 40 stations were crap. If I did turn over to the radio, I kept it on KZEW because the Zoo played deep cuts, none of that pop music pablum.

I wore Dickies khaki pants and flannel shirts in the winter, like Kerouac and Neil Young. In the summer, which in Texas is most of the time, I wore cutoffs and concert t-shirts.

I was the boss of me. I was in control of my style, music, and the art I was exposed to. Pop culture was for the weak minded. Pop culture was for frat boys, preppies and the idiot lemmings who mindlessly followed what Madison Avenue shit down their throats.

I did what I liked, and as I pleased.

In October of 1983, Bob Dylan released Infidels. It was great, the best new Dylan in years. On the album cover, which was important in those days, Dylan wore a slick pair of Wayfarers. In 1983 Raybans, especially Wayfarers, were old man sunglasses. They hadn't been in style since the Eisenhower administration.

But. Dylan. They looked cool on Dylan.

I immediately asked my mamaw for a pair. They were expensive and I was a college kid with no room in the budget for anything except beer, albums, and cassette tapes. She sprung for a pair as a Christmas present and I was in heaven. I was now officially Dylan, Young, and Kerouac cool.

I received some odd looks. One time on campus a frat rat said to me, 'dude, the 1950's called, they want their sunglasses back.' His friends all laughed. I wore it like a badge.

And then springtime 1984 rolled around. Glorious springtime in Texas. Bluebonnets and clear skies. One day I drove out to lake Benbrook, top down on the Spitfire, American Stars and Bars blaring on the cassette player, my long hair blowing in the wind, and of course, I wore the Wayfarers. I pulled up to Mustang Park, got out, reached in the back, pulled out my unecologically friendly Styrofoam cooler (it was the 80s, what the hell did we know) filled with bock, turned around, and look out over a beach full of frat boys wearing Jantzen swim trunks, and Wayfarer sunglasses. My Wayfarer sunglasses. Every dang one of them. What the hell.

I went slack-jawed and stupefied.

Let me jump back to 1983. In August of 1983, three months before Infidels was released, a little movie starring Rebecca De Mornay and a young, unknown actor named Tom Cruise opened to little fanfare and even less expectations. It was called Risky Business. It did alright. I saw it but paid little attention.

Here's the problem. The film launched Tom Cruise into the teenybopper stratosphere. On the poster for the film Cruise was peering over the top of a pair of, you guessed it, Rayban Wayfarers. Over the next six months his face was plastered on every teen, fashion, and film magazine on the planet. Every month, usually on the cover, and usually he was wearing Rayban Wayfarers. I did not read teen, fashion, or film magazines. I did not know he was the new Hollywood heartthrob.

There was no internet in 1983. There was no social media. No streaming bombardment of pop culture. Compared to present day, if you really wanted to avoid that shit, like I did, you could do so pretty easily.

Until it got all up in your face on Mustang Beach.

I was pissed.

I stood there for five minutes, looking at all the frat rats and sorority girls frolicking and drinking on the beach. I started counting the guys in Wayfarers. I stopped when I reached double digits. They were everywhere. Hanging out wearing Izod, Polo, Forenza, Panama Jack, OP, and ogling girls wearing Esprit, Guess, Jordache, and Body Glove.

I threw up in my mouth, put the cooler back in the car, got in, and drove away. On the drive home I pulled into a convenience store and bought a $2.00 pair of plastic sunglasses. I put the Wayfarers in what passed for a glove box in the Spitfire.

Tom Cruise can kiss my ass.

I was to graduate in May of 1984. Six weeks before I was set to walk the stage my ma-maw got T-boned on her way home from grocery shopping. She was pretty banged up, but the doctors seemed to think she would recover. The yellow Malibu she drove, which I coveted, was totaled. It was a scare, but everything seemed fine. I admit to being somewhat relieved that it looked unlikely she would be recovered enough by graduation to make the trip from Denton to Sherman. I knew if she came, she would be looking for me to be wearing the Wayfarers, but no way in hell I was wrapping those preppy glasses around my noggin. Luckily, she was unable to make the ceremony and my rebellious pride remained unscathed.

I graduated and returned home to Fort Worth, ready to start my new adult life. Well, not really, I poked around looking for jobs, but no one was hiring screenwriters in Fort Worth, Texas in 1984. Hell, no one in Fort Worth is hiring screenwriters in 2019. No matter. I caught wind of a screenwriting class being offered at the studios in Los Colinas, about an hour from Fort Worth. I signed up and plunked down a wad of my graduation money. Two six-hour days of intense screenwriting emersion. Saturday was great, I learned a lot, and I was halfway to Los Colinas Sunday morning when I realized I had left my materials back at the house. I could either be on time, without my notes and materials, or go back and arrive late, but prepared. I turned around and drove back home.

When I rushed in the back door, I stopped dead in my tracks. My girlfriend was standing in the middle of the living room, tears streaming down her face and a look of stark terror in her big brown eyes.

"What's wrong," I asked.

"Thank god you came back," she said. She ran to me and threw her arms around my neck.

"What the hell is wrong?" I reiterated.

"Your mom called, not five minutes after you left," my girlfriend broke down sobbing, unable to continue speaking.

"And..."

"Your mamaw is in the hospital in Denton," my girlfriend broke down again. I just stood there, trying to comprehend. Catching her breath, she continued. "Your mamaw collapsed early this morning. They rushed her to the hospital. She is unconscious. In a coma. No brain activity."

She was speaking like a telegraph communique, but that was fine. I was going into shock myself and likely could not have understood complex sentences even if my girlfriend had been able to string them together.

"You were gone. I didn't know where," now her sobs were interrupted by gasping breaths. "I mean, (gasp) I knew where. (gasp) But Los Colinas is a big place. (gasp, gasp) I didn't know where in Los Colinas. I was so scared." She damn near went limp in my arms.

"Oh, baby," I said. Truth be told, I'm not sure I was consoling her or myself.

We stood in the middle of the living room, holding each other for an indeterminable amount of time. Finally, she lifted her head from my chest and said, "You have to go to Denton," she pounded my heart with her fist, "right now."

I kissed her and left.

Denton is a fifty-minute drive from Fort Worth. I pulled into the hospital parking lot in less than twenty minutes. I'll skip the family angst and drama of the day. Enough to say the evening ended with me and my uncle sitting on either side of my mamaw, his mother, as she slowly stopped breathing. Sometimes I still hear the heart monitor flatline in my dreams, and on occasion, even when I'm awake, like a nightmare tinnitus.

The sun was going down when I left the hospital that evening. Sitting in my Spitfire, the world awash in the orange, yellow, and purple of a Texas sunset. I looked over at my glovebox and realized I wasn't my own man. I had let those frat rats dictate what I wore. But I wasn't going to let them rob me of something important to me, the last gift from my mamaw. I reached over and pulled my Wayfarers out of the glovebox. I slid them on and headed into the thickening darkness towards home.

Fuck Tom Cruise.

I was my mamaw's man.

JOSH OLSEN
To BUNT, or not to BUNT

On July 28, 2019, I downloaded Topps BUNT, a digital baseball card trading app. This was far from the first time I downloaded this particular app, but I had previously sworn to myself that this was something I'd never do again. I couldn't remember exactly how long it had been since I last opened BUNT on my phone but based on the purchase history in my Google Play account, I figured it hadn't been since about September 23, 2017. Or at least that was the last time I made an in-app purchase in BUNT.

On September 23, 2017, I purchased a "Rookie Pack Deal" for $0.99. Three days before, on September 20, 2017, I bought a "9th Inning Deal" for $9.99. And on September 15, 2017, five days before that, I bought yet another "9th Inning Deal" for $9.99. And that was far from the start of it. Going back to June 21, 2014, my shameful Google Play purchase history is full of purchases from Topps BUNT and myriad other digital trading card apps.

It all started with BUNT, the digital baseball card trading app, to which I was first introduced thanks to a June 2014 article on Beckett.com, the official website of the most prominent trading card price guide known to all humankind. At first, like with all other "FREE-mium" apps, I was perfectly happy ripping free packs of digital baseball cards using my daily log-on bonus. Sometimes I'd even go a few days without opening a pack. I'd merely log-on, collect my daily coin bonus (the currency used in BUNT), trade a few baseball cards (my favorite component of the app), play in a couple low-stakes fantasy baseball-like games, and then log-off. I'd occasionally rip a pack and pull an insert, which I could then flip for rarer, more desirable cards, but mostly I was content with trading cards in order to build my collection of Detroit Tigers, as well as my all-time favorite baseball player/celebrity persona since 1989, "Mr. 40/40" himself, Jose Canseco. BUNT provided me with almost all of the joy of collecting baseball cards, ripping packs, trading cards, building a personal collection, but without any of the expense or space limitations.

But clearly, I didn't remain content with the free aspect of the app for very long.

It began slowly, buying a $0.99 "Bonus Pack" here and there. But soon I realized that if you had any serious desire to collect inserts or player signatures (digital autographs on digital baseball cards), the hardest of all cards to collect, you really had no choice but to purchase additional coins. And so, buy I did.

For almost the next three years, I purchased an embarrassing amount of coins from BUNT, or at least the amount is embarrassing to me. In reality, any amount spent in a digital trading card app should be embarrassing, even if it's just $0.99. But it wasn't just the in-app purchases that lead me to delete BUNT from my phone. It was my obsession with BUNT, and all other digital trading card apps, that forced me to eventually swear off all digital trading cards.

Not long after I first downloaded BUNT, I also downloaded HUDDLE, the Topps football card app, which didn't take up much more of my time, because I've never been a fan of football. But what this did allow is for something the BUNT community referred to as "cross trading:" that is, organizing deals with fellow app community members in which you trade digital cards in one app for digital cards in another wholly separate app. Never mind that both apps were properties of Topps (the only current baseball card manufacturer producing MLB licensed cards). Cross trading was explicitly forbidden from these apps, and while most cross traders were honest and relatively fair, although baseball cards were typically seen as more valuable than football, or any other type of digital trading card, you always ran the risk of running across scammers, or members who agree to a cross trade, accept the cards they want on one app, and then deny or ignore the trade that would benefit you. Being that cross trading was not allowed in these apps, in the first place, it meant that there was no real consequence for such actions. You could complain and call names in the comment section of the apps, which occurred rather frequently, but it typically accomplished little more than possibly earning a suspension (temporary) or ban (permanent) from said app, especially if the scorned member resorted to curse words, although most were automatically censored within the app (even creative spellings of swear words were flagged).

Well, in my case, along with who knows how many members of the BUNT community, downloading BUNT was a gateway to HUDDLE (football), which lead to KICK (soccer), which lead to Star Wars Card Trader, which lead to KNOCKOUT (UFC), which lead to The Walking Dead Card Trader, which lead to SLAM (WWE), an app that miraculously featured digital autographs of long-deceased professional wrestlers, such as Andre the Giant and "Macho Man" Randy Savage. But these were only the Topps licensed digital trading card apps. I also downloaded Kitty Cards and Trump Cards, which were, as you probably guessed, digital trading cards of kittens (aww) and Donald Trump (gag), along with the other 2016 presidential candidates. I rather quickly lost interest in just about all of these apps, with the exception of BUNT and SLAM, but still, I kept up with the other apps in order to make cross trades for BUNT and SLAM.

I even had duplicate or "alt" accounts for several of the apps, which were basically dummy accounts used for hoarding and "harvesting" coins (also prohibited in the app terms and conditions). So, in addition to maintaining my primary app accounts, I would open my alt accounts, hoard coins from the daily log-on bonus, rip packs, and if I pulled an insert, trade it to my main account. And yes, of course that eventually lead to purchasing coins in my alt accounts, as well, because spenders receive VIP perks, including "free" bonus cards which I could then trade for other cards I actually wanted (like Cansecos). But my spending didn't stop there.

Not only did I purchase physical Topps baseball cards, which were packaged along with randomly inserted BUNT promotional codes, but I occasionally resorted to the most shameful of all digital trading card app practices, and actually bought digital cards on eBay.

In addition to cross trading, alt accounts, and harvesting coins, buying and selling digital cards on a third-party platform like eBay was strictly prohibited, and could result in the suspension or ban of either the seller or buyer of these cards, and not unlike cross trading, buyers of digital cards were also vulnerable to scamming. But at least in the case of eBay, if a buyer did ever get scammed, eBay would hold the seller accountable, to the best of their abilities. BUNT, however, would look the other way … unless they just decided to ban you.

I never got suspended or banned from BUNT or any other digital trading card app. I was always a friendly and enthusiastic member. If anything, I was too enthusiastic. I never calculated exactly how much money I spent on trading card apps like BUNT and SLAM, and I can't bring myself to do it right here and now (because then I would have no choice but to publish my grand total for all to see), but I would easily estimate that it was in the hundreds. Granted, a few hundred dollars over the span of three years might not seem like much to spend on a hobby/obsession. I mean, many people spend a few hundred dollars on tangible, print baseball cards (if not one card) in a single day. But my spending habits were something I kept hidden from my family. My partner would often see me on my phone and tablet, playing around with my line-ups and ripping packs in BUNT, and tease me about how much time I spent on there, but she had no idea (until now) that I was spending money, real money, our money, on digital trading cards, and she truly had no idea how much time I was spending on those apps.

And that - not only the money, but the time and deception behind it all - was ultimately what convinced me to swear off BUNT.

Swear it off, that is, until the night of July 28, 2019.

What can I say? The Detroit Tigers were the worst team in baseball, local sports radio was full of talk of the looming trade deadline, and in a moment of weakness/late night boredom, my curiosity got the best of me. I wanted to see what BUNT 2019 looked like (I had successfully skipped 2018 altogether). I wanted to see if I could still access my collection. I wanted to see my precious, pristine Cansecos. So, I downloaded BUNT, and for the first time in almost two years, I opened the app.

Hey, I had 44,000 coins left in my account!

This was likely my way of leaving a little something stashed away in the off-chance that I ever came back to the app, so I immediately started ripping packs. I told myself that I'd only keep the app on my phone for as long as it took me to write this essay, but my 44,000 coins were long gone before I finished a first draft, and there were so many new Cansecos to add to my collection.

MATT SPRINGER
Time to Match the Stars

During the summer of 1989, two things fascinated me. One was Tim Burton's *Batman*. The other was *Match Game*.

Every morning at eleven, I'd sit myself down in front of the television to watch Ross Shaffer shepherd an aging Charles Nelson Reilly and five other celebs through a half-hour of banter, schtick and bits--with the occasional game show competition thrown in for good measure. (This was long before Alec Baldwin got his grubby paws on the show.) As an impressionable pre-teen with an abiding obsession for That Business We Call Show, I thought it was just about the most entertaining thing I'd ever seen.

Of course, I'd always been a game show fan--among my earliest words were "A brand new car!"--but this was something different. This was more than just the vicarious thrill of watching someone pick up fabulous prizes as a well-endowed model preened. No, this was like gaining entrance into some secret society.

For a half-hour every day, I was admitted into the elite club known as

Celebrity. I could watch six "stars" casually toss around one-liners and needle each other as though they were sipping martinis at the Copa and not on a soundstage. I didn't feel like I was at home on my couch with a bowl of cereal and the constant distraction of my budding crush on Jenny Szabo. I felt like I was in that studio audience--or even better, on that panel of stars, whipping out goofy answers with the best of them. It was then that I began to understand what it means to be appreciated not because you are talented, but simply because you are famous.

Later, I discovered the roots of this bastardized version of *Match Game* in the endless reruns of the classic seventies *Match Game* on Game Show Network. I have a soft spot in my heart for my *Match Game*, but the original is drinking from the source, seminal episodes in trash culture history that are clearly superior to their late-eighties counterpart.

For the uninitiated, a brief tutorial. On *Match Game*, two contestants (usually one middle-aged fella and a cute housewife or college student) must provide a word or phrase to complete a "blank" in a sentence, most often a mildly suggestive joke. For example, "Freida said, 'I hate being married to an umpire. Every night when I get into bed, he screams, BLANK.'" If your suggestion to fill that blank ("Yer out!" or "Ball!") matches one of the answers chosen by one of the six celebrities, you get a point. The person with the most points after three rounds goes on to the Big Money Match, where they can spin the Star Wheel and have one shot to win as much as $20,000.

On the surface, just another game show. But oh, so much more.

Most of the credit has to go to the "panel of stars," the six celebrities who in each episode attempt to match their answers with the contestants. Though there was a constant rotation of semi-regulars and one-time visitors to the *Match Game* panel, the anchor of the show revolves around three panelists--Richard Dawson, Brett Sommers and Charles Nelson Reilly.

Dawson would move over to the *Match Game* "spin-off" *Family Feud* in the late seventies, a show that would eventually surpass *Match Game* in popularity. But he fine-tuned his swingin' horny guy persona on *Match Game*. It simply isn't a true *Match Game* episode unless Richard has made some suggestive comment to a contestant, a fellow panelist, or even host Gene Rayburn. The man was a taut bundle of fuck.

Brett and Charles (or Chuck, as he is often known on the show) took a more gentle approach to the game. Occupying the center and stage left spots on the upper tier for most episodes, they're the Burns and Allen of the *Match Game* stage. In fact, it's often hard to tell which one's Burns and which one's Allen as they riff their way through each half-hour in a constant effort to crack each other up.

Of the two, Brett was typically the more involved player, always ready with a quip for a contestant--in one episode of *Match Game PM*, the bawdier evening counterpart to the daytime edition, she even tries to set up a single male contestant with occasional panelist Marcia Wallace, former supporting player on *The Bob Newhart Show* and the voice of Mrs. Krabappel on *The Simpsons*.

In contrast, Charles lives up to his raging queen persona by being hilariously catty, mocking and even flirtatious. In one episode, when former *Laugh-In* co-host Dick Martin mentions that he's "going to go with Big Chuck" and give the same answer as him, Charles replies, "Most men do, Dick." An unsung master of comic timing, he'll sit quietly on that upper tier for long stretches of the show, smirking and silently observing the action, then let loose with a perfectly- timed joke that brings the house down. Charles can also be spotted occasionally jotting down private jokes on the *Match Game* cards for Brett's enjoyment, and you'll frequently hear her nicotine-drenched laugh echo out over jokes that have been forever lost to the mists of time.

Many of the semi-regular panelists--Avery Schreiber, Marcia Wallace, Betty White--bring their own ingredients to the chemical mix. But it's really Richard Dawson, Brett Sommers and Charles Nelson Reilly around which the show's dynamic was built. You also can't deny the contributions of Gene Rayburn, who let loose with his own steady stream of passable one-liners, but his role more often than not is that of bemused ringleader and straight man.

Looking at that roster of names, you might be hard-pressed to decipher what most of the panelists were even famous for, other than appearing on *Match Game*. Reilly had a supporting role on *The Ghost and Mrs.*

Muir, a mostly-forgotten two-season sitcom based on the film of the same name. Dawson spent several seasons on *Hogan's Heroes*. Sommers is best known as the perennially separated wife of *Odd Couple* star Jack Klugman.

And yet, they sit regularly on a "panel of stars." These are people who are famous for being famous; in their way, they predicted the reality-rampant rise of the modern professional celebrity.

In that sense, it's gloriously terrible television, because it's the worst thing entertainment can be: self-indulgent. Why should we care to watch six nobodies who act like somebodies get soused as they try not to screw our fellow lumpenproletariats out of game show swag?

I do care, and it pains me to realize why. I think I genuinely like these people. In its most relaxed moments, there's an intimacy to *Match Game* where I really do feel like I'm in on some private joke shared by the panelists. It might be the first-- or only? --game show in which I feel like I'm encouraged to identify with the celebrities and not with the contestants. Any fool can travel from Biloxi for a shot at twenty grand, but I don't need that. I want to kibitz with Charles and Brett, get leeringly winked at by Richard Dawson and cut in front of Marcia Wallace at the craft services buffet.

On some level, I understand what *Match Game* really is-- six celebs and Gene Rayburn barely involved in the game, getting lightly toasted and trying to entertain each other, while a steady stream of average folk trot across the stage hoping to win what is commonly known in the game show biz as "the big money." And yet, I can't help feeling that something died with the classic *Match Game* of the seventies and early eighties. Our understanding of that mysterious beast known as "celebrity" has transformed.

These days, we still care about who Taylor Swift is dating and what George Clooney is gonna name his kids. But our tolerance has diminished. Were they suddenly to appear each night on our television drunk and schticking it up, we'd simply change the channel. Instead, our appetite for "reality" has become insatiable; we'll gladly watch Khloe Kardashian pick her navel lint instead. Heck, we can't even tolerate the Oscars anymore--everyone's always bitching about how long the show is. Back in the *Match Game* days, we'd be thrilled about four hours of celeb-watching and schmooze. Now we balk.

I do love a frequent suckle off the reality TV teat, but I'll always remain fond of my reruns of classic *Match Game* and continue watching that panel of third-rate stars go through the motions--not because I can identify with them at all, but because I can't. I don't really want to be them. I just want to be their friend.

KYLE STEDMAN
Drenched in 1988

What draws us to one place and not another, what force or magnetism pulls us back and forth across continents and oceans to settings that for seemingly unexplained or unexplainable reasons speak to our inner selves, our need?

—Dan Wakefield, *Returning* (March 1988)

January

In the 1988 comedy *Tapeheads*, a mustachioed John Cusack celebrates his coworker Tim Robbins' birthday by throwing a party for him in the building they're supposed to be security-guarding. The party is 80s-big: there's horn-heavy, synthy dance music and graffiti and leather skirts and skateboarding and red lipstick on the security camera lens. "Don't you think this is getting out of hand?" asks Robbins. Cusack responds, "Yeah, don't mention it!"

My 1988 experiment started like that: a playful way to push expectations, a party I threw myself for no reason but the pleasure of it. I wanted to dive as deep as possible into 1988, knowing that if anyone thought I was going too far, I'd just respond like Cusack: "Yeah, don't mention it!"

The idea was simple: in each month of 2018, I'd experience as much as possible of that same month in 1988—the movies, the books, the music, the TV, the history. So, in January I listened to Taylor Dayne and The Pogues, I read Rebecca Ore's novel *Becoming Alien*, I watched a January 1988 episode of *Cheers*, and I watched Molly Ringwald in *For Keeps*. They were all in the air at the same time exactly thirty years earlier, at the same cultural moment, like the various atoms making up the smells drifting from an easy-bake oven.

I'm not really sure why. Born in 1980, I remember some of 1988 but not much. I wasn't trying to draw conclusions about the past or learn lessons from history; it was more like taking a bath in an entire year, letting its pop culture soak into my ears and over my submerged face, leaving a soapy residue that wouldn't easily rinse off.

February

But just two months into 2018/1988, things took a turn I hadn't expected; I could hear Tim Robbins asking me, "Don't you think this is getting out of hand?"

I tried to explain it to my wife Margo. "So, two of the movies that came out at the beginning of 1988 were both about young people struggling to be parents," I said. We were laying around having quiet reading time, drinking tea.

She looked up from her book, so I continued. "*For Keeps* is this really depressing movie about trying to raise a baby before you've even finished high school. It came out in January 1988. And then in February in *She's Having a Baby*, Kevin Bacon is married to Elizabeth McGovern, and they're trying to get pregnant for a while. Then they have the kid and then life is hard for *them*, too." I shifted positions on the couch, facing her more fully. "It was in the air or something—this idea of how hard it is to raise kids without starving or alienating your family."

Margo said, "Maybe it's the universe trying to tell you something. Like, since we're not having our own bio-kids—maybe you're being drawn to movies on that topic." She smiled, gently joking, but knowing that I'd savor the idea of 1988 having cosmic importance.

We both turned back to our books—mine, Ian McDonald's February 1988 *Desolation Road*—but my mind wasn't on it. The sound of the two movies was still echoing in my ears, but now with a new motif added: our own childlessness.

*

Ringwald's performance of postpartum depression in *For Keeps* is hard to watch. It feels unfair that her body is betraying her after she fought so hard to have her child. She's like a soldier who escaped captivity only to develop an infection on the hike back home.

Margo's body treated her unfairly too. In early 2017, after years of a ballooning sickness, She had a surgery that healed her but left us sure we wouldn't have biological kids. And though we were surprised—we'd always expected children to come eventually—we weren't devastated. Unless we adopted, we'd be childless. That was okay. This was a new pool to swim around in, feeling the edges, testing the depths. But it was comfortable, warm.

Every few weeks, we'd say to each other, "Should we foster? Should we adopt? Should we host orphans from overseas?" The answer was always, "Maybe. Not yet. Maybe?"

Once we were cleaning the bathroom together, and I confessed that I didn't really want to adopt, but that I felt guilty saying so out loud. I scrubbed the sink harder.

"I feel the same way," said Margo, catching my eye in the mirror's reflection. "And you know what's a really bad motivation when making a decision that big? Guilt."

March

In March 1988, *Beetlejuice* hit theaters. One website critiques the film's assumptions about parenthood, saying it "reads like a foreign adoption story about a childless couple wandering the earth until they are made into a real family via the addition of a child." And that's how it felt when I watched it in March 2018: Margo and I were Alec Baldwin and Geena Davis, ghosts, alone in a historic house. The movie seemed to say that if we adopted (perhaps a young Winona Ryder), we'd feel more solid.

But consider the case of Netflix's *Stranger Things* (set in the 80s, if not created then). Here too is Winona Ryder, that dancing child from *Beetlejuice*, now grown and a parent to her own on-screen child Will, who always ends up missing or possessed or screaming. Imagine that Ryder is really playing the same character—that the young Lydia from *Beetlejuice* changed her name to Joyce and moved to Hawkins, Indiana, where she had a couple kids and settled down. On one hand, think how perfectly equipped she would be to accept the supernatural events from *Stranger Things*: "I've seen ghosts before, so I can handle it," she might think to herself, off camera.

But on the other hand, think how unfair it would be for her to return to the world of the undead, of monsters, of hauntings. "I've seen ghosts before," she might think at other times, "so I shouldn't have to go through it again."

Put differently: as a gothy 13-year-old in *Beetlejuice*, she tells her parents, "My whole life is a dark room" as a badge, a declaration of style. But in *Stranger Things*, I wonder if she whispers "My whole life is a dark room" whenever she cries over her afflicted son.

And watching Ryder's character in *Stranger Things*, *I guiltily asked myself, How could parenting be worth this anguish?*

*

"When will you die?" sings Morrisey repeatedly in "Margaret on the Guillotine," the final track of *Viva Hate*, his March 1988 solo debut.

What an odd phrase, *solo debut*: a celebration of aloneness.

*

The same month *Beetlejuice* was released, Doris Lessing published *The Fifth Child*, a novel about a happy couple who is advised repeatedly to stop having kids. "People are brainwashed into believing family life is the best," says one of the in-laws. The lovers disagree and continue building their family, but their fifth child is an unexpected terror—a violent, odd boy whose siblings fear him.

Reading this, after yet another trip to the library in search of novels from 1988, I remembered taking baths with my siblings as a young child, and how we'd scratch each other's backs as a game. "Turn around!" one would yell, and all three of us would turn, water splashing everywhere. Everyone was a receiver, and everyone gave.

But my younger brother Phillip never quite understood the game. Not quite two years younger than me, it was always clear that he was different—not talking quite clearly as a child, a scar on his chest from his heart surgery as an infant, not ready for school yet. And in the tub, he scratched hard enough to draw blood.

April

In April 1988, Michael J. Fox starred in *Bright Lights, Big City* as an upward-climbing, coke-addicted yuppie in 80s New York City.

I watched it on a cloudy Saturday morning in April 2018, curled on my couch drinking coffee, partly because I like Fox's acting and partly because it was one of the only April 88 films on a streaming service I was already paying for. And there was the parenting theme again—by then, I was starting to assume I'd accidentally discover a parenting movie for every month of 1988.

Fox's character is obsessed with a tabloid story about a pregnant woman in a coma; he's haunted by images of the baby refusing to be born. We eventually learn that he's mourning the death of his own mother, traumatic memories we experience through quick, unexplained flashbacks: there she is in a hospital bed, flash, now it's more cocaine and parties.

And the flashes feel just right, how the memory of pain can flash into view in an unexpected instant, as if an eye doctor sat us down and pressed our faces against his cold, metal phoropter and flipped between different lenses—A or B, life or pain—and thus changed our entire perception for a moment before nonchalantly flipping us back to where we were, breathless, everything out of focus.

That Saturday morning on the couch, Fox's flashes to hospital scenes at first reminded me of my wife's hospital visits: a flash to the day our new, lost kitten was stuck outside in the snow when we had to leave for the hospital; how Margo sobbed and shook her head and clenched my hand during one invasive procedure; how I cried in the shower, leaning my head against the cold tiles, that first time I imagined cleaning out her closet if I lost her, gasping for air at the impossibility of it.

But those flashes passed quickly; I had dealt with them through counseling and conversation, so they didn't linger. Instead, the film's memory-flashes brought me unexpectedly to another hospital room: my brother Phillip's.

*

In early 2017, a year and change before I watched *Bright Lights*, I flew to Orlando to visit Phillip, who was once again in the hospital with complications from Crohn's disease—the most recent of a decade of hospital stays.

But this time was different. In the ICU, he looked (and I feel guilty even writing this) like a movie monster that the audience is supposed to halfway fear and halfway pity, like a Dalek on *Doctor Who* when the metal exterior is opened, and we see the sad fetus-squid within. Phillip had a breathing tube down his throat, and his hands were in huge gloves to keep him from pulling it out on the rare occasion he woke up from his drugs enough to grasp and flail in terror, his roving, bloodshot eyes panning back and forth across the room. I stood by him, my hand touching the scabby red skin of his arm, not knowing when to look at him and when to look away. The machine breathed for him like a broken furnace.

He was like that for three days. But he improved on the fourth, just before I flew back home to Illinois. The breathing tube was out, he was less drugged than before, and surprising me, he made his usual jokes. A fourth-grader's mind was in his rebellious, thirty-four-year-old body, and even now, surfacing his head from days of underwater haze, he used the same funny repeated phrases he had loved since his 80s childhood: he spread his arms to "present" the chair next to me as if he were Vanna White, stuck out his tongue, and told me I was under arrest if I didn't sit next to him. This was all for the ritual of watching *The Price is Right*, his favorite show for as long as I can remember.

That's my best, last memory of him on that trip: he held a beloved Matchbox car tight in each hand, with a solid, closed-lips grin unflinchingly on his face as he watched the hospital TV with all his attention, overjoyed to be himself again, like a stone that has been rolled back to the position it was meant to be in.

*

It was probably a little after 1988 when our adult family friend Bob visited our house to use me and my friend Ben as actors in his homemade *Star Trek* movie. I played Captain Kirk, Ben played Dr. McCoy, and we walked around our backyard delivering odd lines into Bob's fancy VHS camcorder.

Phillip wanted to be involved but was too young to consistently deliver speaking lines, so he was cast as the monster. Bob wrapped him up in a thick Mexican blanket so only his face emerged. Phillip then stared into the distance and said a generic "Rawr, rawr, rawr"—I always think of this when I see Pizza the Hutt in *Spaceballs*—and I overacted my response just right: "My God, Bones—what is that *thing*?"

As a kid, I knew Phillip had some kind of mental disability, but this movie costume matched how I treated him at my worst: as an object I could wrap up and manipulate and feed lines to and not really bother to understand that much.

Years later, on the Saturday morning I watched Michael J. Fox snort all that cocaine in *Bright Lights*, I was wrapped up in the same Mexican blanket that turned Phillip into an alien. Perhaps I pulled it tight so only my face peeked out. "Rawr, rawr," I said to no one in particular.

*

In the April 1988 novel *Master of the Return* by Tova Reich, an elderly midwife grows younger and younger while delivering a child: "The skin at her throat no longer sagged; teeth flashed in her gums; her hair shone rich and dark."

But I can't help wondering, what about those who daily witness not the coming of life but the coming of death—nurses, doctors, volunteers? Do they age *faster* than the rest of us, one year older for each step they take toward the deafening machines crying out from every room in the ICU?

May

As an adult, I spoke more with Phillip than with anyone else in my family. He called every day or two, eager to share news about Uncle Ron's new car or the gator attack in Kissimmee or to ask what sorts of things my new cat had done lately. ("That darn cat!" he'd giggle every time he mentioned her, the joke just as funny to him every time he said it.) I don't think I ever told him that Margo and I wouldn't have kids, but I doubt he would have believed me if I had; I imagine his voice saying, "You'd better tell me the truth or you're under arrest!"

Some days I enjoyed the attention, the updates, the joy that can't help but seep into you when someone seeks you out. To Phillip, we were still playing in the bathtub, splashing and joking, and often I verbally splashed him back, smiling. But sometimes I blew him off, letting his call go to voicemail (prompting him to leave the same, nearly verbatim message he left last time, always ending with "I love you and God bless"). I figured there was no need to call him back, since he would surely try again in a few hours.

By May 2018, I knew I'd see something about childlessness or Phillip's illness in every 1988 book I read. It was almost a challenge: I'd pick up C.J. Cherryh's *Cyteen* from the library and glare at it, sitting like a brick on the passenger seat of my car, daring it to preach at me about whether or not I should have children, how exactly I should feel about my brother.

The science fiction novel *Cyteen* centers on two boys, raised as brothers. One is a clone of the father, and one is conditioned to be a servant, like a human computer. Despite their differences, they love each other unconditionally, going to the utmost risk to save each other from danger.

Bored, I skimmed the last few pages quickly, trying to get it back to the library as quickly as possible.

June

The 2nd highest-grossing film of 1988 was June's *Who Framed Roger Rabbit*, a film about hardened detective Eddie Valiant trying to deal with his fun-loving brother's death.

In June 1988, I was seven, and I was pretty often annoyed with five-year-old Phillip. He loved playing with cars and riding bikes, and so did I, but he couldn't sit still for the TV shows I wanted to watch (*Muppet Babies, Pee-Wee's Playhouse*), and he never stopped talking. He followed me everywhere, a Matchbox car clutched in each hand. If I got up in the night to pee, he was outside the door when I opened it again, unable to lay in bed when *something was happening somewhere* that he wasn't witnessing.

I don't remember if I saw *Roger Rabbit* in the theater, but if I did, I would have felt a connection with Eddie and his struggles with Roger Rabbit. Here was Eddie, trying to live his life on his own terms, and he was forced to put up with this intense character who bounced off the walls with energy, sang at the top of his lungs, wouldn't leave his side, and never stopped talking.

Watching *Roger Rabbit* in 2018, I still empathized with Eddie, and partly because of his relationship with the Phillip-like Roger. But by now, there was that other side of Eddie to connect with: the part of him that lost a brother.

July

In July 1988, Alice Hoffman's novel *At Risk* was published. Polly, the elder of two child siblings, contracts AIDs from a blood transfusion. Her younger brother Charlie deals with her gradual illness by disappearing into nature and watching a pond for a huge turtle that he hopes to capture on film. He surveys the pond through a camera lens, through which "things look more yellow than they are. Shadows seem darker, more permanent." Hoffman then immediately, in the next sentences, moves from the experience of seeing life through a lens to the experience of losing a sibling: "Charlie will never let himself forget her," Hoffman writes. "Not in a million years."

Phillip died in March 2017. On his birthday seven months later, I rode my bike into the October twilight. At the end of the trail were a group of horses behind a fence. Remembering that *Phillip* means *lover of horses*, I watched them for a while, trying to make friends, willing them to accept my love. I took some pictures, but eventually I put my phone away so there wouldn't be anything between us. Soon afterward, I decided to experience 1988 throughout the following year—a decision that probably wasn't related to Phillip's death, but I can't really say for sure.

"Don't let it ever be October," Polly says to herself in *At Risk*, wanting to hold onto as much life as she can. "Go backward, through August, July, June, May, and April. We don't care if we ever see Autumn again."

August / September

By August and September of 2018, I was convinced that 1988 wasn't anything special. We all have baggage about those who parented us or who we'll parent; we've all lost people; we all yearn for lost siblings, no matter how little time we actually spent understanding them. That must be the stuff of all texts, of all films, from all years, not just 1988. It's just up to us to notice it, to scribble lines between the dots.

So really, do you need to hear the litany of parenting stories I experienced as the summer ended? Just summarizing them makes them start to sound the same: in *Married to the Mob*, Michelle Pfeiffer sacrifices everything to protect her son. In *Running on Empty*, another mom sacrifices everything to protect *her* son. In Sherri Tepper's novel *The Gate to Women's Country*, mothers are separated from their male children, who might or might not choose to return to them after an adolescence away. In Anne Tyler's novel *Breathing Lessons*, a mother tries to micromanage her distant son and grandchild. It's all mothers, fathers, parents, families, all the time. And that's just two months' worth of the 1988 stories I saw and read.

And those parenting stories got easier to hear: I stopped feeling an empathetic identification with fictional mothers and fathers, wasn't daydreaming about how much I would or wouldn't sacrifice for a child, how micromanage-y I might or might not be. Margo and I still checked in with each other: *We're still okay, right? Just us, and the cat? Loving our nieces, nephews, the children of close friends, but from a distance, not as parents? Yes?*

Yes. In September, we hosted two of our young godchildren for the weekend. Taking our role as fun aunt and uncle seriously, we petted animals and frolicked at a festival and read stories and splashed in the bath and ate sweets. Before Margo and I turned off the light at night, we smiled at each other, holding hands in bed. We delivered the kids back to their parents on Sunday, proud of giving them a good time, but not regretting the return to our regular life.

Yes. Our lives are good. It's a bit of a stretch to say specifically that it's these 1988 stories that convinced me that parenting is too hard, that it's not worth the pain or the possibility of loss. And it's not like those fears are the sum total of our decision not to parent; there are plenty of other reasons too. But it's not quite accurate to say the 1988 stories *aren't* part of our contentment, either. We step into the future holding hands, proud of where we've been and where we're going.

*

It was January 2017 when Margo and I knew for sure that we wouldn't have biological children and began to suspect that we wouldn't adopt, and it was two months later when we lost Phillip. Another way of putting it: as I grew to accept that I wasn't willing to face the losses inherent in parenting, my parents lost their son. ("If you've never wept and want to, have a child," wrote David Foster Wallace many years after 1988.)

I remember sitting at Phillip's memorial service and hearing someone on the stage say that loss isn't a momentary glitch in the general joyfulness of life; instead, loss *is* life. It's not something to run from, but to expect. It's an exercise, a muscle you build by swimming daily in that pool, mourning with hope instead of despair, with faith, as much as you're able to. At least, that's the theory I heard at the service and subscribe to still, however bad I am at living it—I mean, as happy as I am about my decision not to parent, I realize there's a part of me trying to control what can't be controlled, avoid what can't be avoided.

Here's the narrator in Lee Smith's *Fair and Tender Ladies* (September 1988): "I have spent half of my life wanting and the other half grieving, and most often I have been wanting and grieving the same thing. There has been precious little in-between."

That helps me see myself through a new lens: the relationships I've wanted—those that never developed as I'd hoped, and those that never came to be—are also the relationships I've grieved and am grieving. There has been precious little in-between.

*

Just three days after Phillip's death, I was at my parents' house scanning photos of him for the memorial service. He was so small for a five-year-old in 1988 and clearly didn't understand the "smile for the camera" convention yet. He's happiest in photos with others, like when he's riding his older cousin Jessica's back. (As I write this, I flash unexpectedly to a memory of his small body sitting on the bottom of a pool, huge eyes open and looking up to the surface, before an adult noticed and dove in to rescue him. Why are memories of joy so often partnered with memories of fear?)

At my parents' house, I opened the computer for a Facebook break and saw that one of my writing professors, Twila Yates Papay, had just passed, probably while I was on the plane, perhaps flying just above her as she left her body.

Twila and Phillip only met each other once or twice, but they both asked about each other regularly. He could tell when someone was genuinely interested in him, when they asked questions and really wanted to hear his answers.

Twila and her husband Joe didn't have children, but they did invite college students over to their house regularly—visits that more than once included awkward performances with their "children": stuffed animals of a kangaroo and an elephant. Imagine twenty-year-olds silently watching 60-somethings use high-pitched, cartoon voices to talk about the sexual positions possible when you have a pouch and a trunk.

After I graduated, I realized that my many invitations to their house were just a small slice of a revolving door of close relationships Twila and Joe had formed over the years, including students, friends, and family. Twila told me story after story of people who moved in and out of their various guest rooms. "Childless" only in the biological sense.

As a graduation gift, Twila unexpectedly gave me a crisp, hardcover set of Susan Cooper's five *The Dark is Rising* books. I was shocked into tears, but she pretended not to notice and said, "You can only take these on one condition: that you read them aloud with Phillip." I murmured something about how we didn't really do that together, but she insisted, and I agreed.

While living at home that summer, I did read Harry Potter out loud with him a couple of times, expecting it to blossom into a new habit, a pattern of us reading all of Potter together and all of the Cooper novels too. But we quickly abandoned it, and I read the books instead in my room, alone on my bed.

October

In Madeleine L'Engle's October 1988 memoir *Two-Part Invention*, she writes, "When I fell on the ice in the woods and broke my shoulder, it hurt …. I don't remember the *feel* of what the pain was like, only that it was intense. Perhaps a psychic blow produces such pain that it, too, is forgotten once it has healed."

November

I once planned to make a mixtape of music inspired by Phillip, which I always knew would include R.E.M.'s "The Wrong Child," from their November 1988 album *Green*.

"I'm not supposed to be like this," sings the isolated narrator repeatedly, asking the other children to accept him despite his differences. Yet he always swims through that despair instead of sinking into it, imploring the listeners, "Let's try to find a happy game to play," and ending the song with "It's okay, okay."

The thing is, the way Michael Stipe sings "okay," it doesn't really sound okay.

December

I watched December 1988's *The Accidental Tourist* late in 2018, after the Christmas tree was up. By now, Margo and I were feeling better than ever about childlessness; we were excited at hosting our nieces in our big, *Beetlejuice*-y house every summer and were regularly crafting plans for loving the other children in our lives. And like Twila, we knew we'd start inviting college students over more often too—my own students, now that I was teaching.

That December, I told Margo about this essay, and I heard a slice of fear in her voice as she said, "You *are* okay not having kids? Right?" And I assured her that yes, I'm the same, we're still looking at life through the same lens, it's just an essay.

In *The Accidental Tourist*, William Hurt and Kathleen Turner are grieving the loss of their son, and of course to me it's about Phillip, too: the stilted conversations among those who loved the dead boy, the unexpected tears when you hug a friend, the dreams when you think he's still alive. In one of mine, Phillip is there in the room with my entire family.

We all know he's dead, even though he's there hanging out with us, but no one has the guts to tell him the truth. In the movie, the loss is driving the parents apart; I often pray a quick prayer of thanks that mine are still together, alive and brave.

And once again: the guilty sigh of relief that I'm never going to face the death of a child.

*

Rain Man swept the Oscars and was the highest-grossing movie of 1988, even though it wasn't released until mid-December. So as the new year approached, I knew *Rain Man* was coming, like a rising tide; I decided early on that it would be my last movie of the year. Despite its popularity, part of me dreaded it. *Rain Man* was a dark pond I couldn't see the bottom of.

Perhaps you remember it: Dustin Hoffman plays Ray, the autistic savant who is always annoying Tom Cruise's character Charlie, the brash and angry brother, the selfish brother, the one who yells.

I don't yell much these days, but I remember yelling. I was probably 13 or 14, and our family was staying in some friend's condo on the beach. Phillip was everywhere: messing with my sand castles, following me on my boogie board, asking me questions while I tried to read my *Star Wars* novel. I finally went inside the condo to get away from him and everyone else in my family, and he followed me. And to scare him off, I yelled at him, as loud as I could, screaming words I've forgotten but which nevertheless had a clear message: *No matter what you want to say, I will outshout you, and I will get the last word, and I hope this frightens you so much that you never try to bother me again.*

He *was* frightened. I think he physically stepped back and held his hands to his face, crying and confused. I was scared too, of what I could become. I've lost my temper since then, but I don't know if I've felt that much shame over an outburst. That shame inspires my current gentleness.

And *Rain Man* was going to remind me of that part of me, I just knew it. Still, the 1988 experiment wouldn't be complete without it. How could I tell friends that I watched something as ridiculous as *Tapeheads* but skipped the biggest movie of the year?

But it wasn't what I expected. Tom Cruise's Charlie is so supercilious and awful that I didn't feel connected to him at all; instead, I was frustrated at how much the film seemed to care about his rehabilitation instead of dropping him at the curb to focus on Ray's growth instead. Sure, there were surprising moments of connection to my life, like how much Ray calms down when he gets a portable TV, just as I saw Phillip relax when he had familiar physical objects in his hands. And I couldn't help but smile at some of Ray's familiar speech habits, like his repetitions. But Ray's repeated words didn't infuriate me, as they did Charlie; they made me smile and remember Phillip.

So instead of watching *Rain Man* through the lens of Charlie, I focused instead on Ray. How he seems distant from the world but is really processing more than most people realize. How if you watch closely, you can see that he's not cold and unemotional but warm and full of love for the people around him, especially his brother, whether the brother deserves that love or not. How he forgives even what shouldn't be forgiven. How his inherent value as a person is broadened further by the impact he has on those around him, which is as weighty and wide as a lake.

I'm also thinking about how I checked out the DVD from the library, and it was so scratched that I had to skip about half an hour near the middle—the part where Charlie is at his most manipulative, using Ray's skill with numbers to make money at casinos, according to the summary I read online. I didn't have to watch Charlie talk Ray into doing things he didn't want to do, as I so often talked to Phillip. So, for me, watching in 2018, those scenes didn't happen; I had to get past the scratches to discover how it ended. And that's like me too, how the scratches on my shiniest surfaces are both part of me and something to push past, as I swim into the future, gulping air before a particularly powerful kick forward.

*

Remember, I was 7 in 1988. So, in 2018, I wasn't visited by flashes of nostalgia when I saw Cruise or Cusack—only when I saw Pee Wee Herman or heard Garfield's cartoon voice. Hearing R.E.M. and Morrisey might bring some people back 30 years, but for me nothing sounds so 1988 as the *DuckTales* theme or the songs from that Paula Abdul tape my sister wore out.

And the toys. Throughout 2018, I would stay awake long after Margo had fallen asleep, propped up on pillows next to her, scrolling on my phone through scans of 1988 catalogs for Lego, Transformers, He-Man— all images that made my hands tingle with the sudden memory of touching those particular plastics. I would gasp as if drowning when I saw photos of Centurion toys, knowing immediately which accessories fit which characters, what kind of clicks sounded, how hard you had to push.

Phillip died with two Matchbox cars in his hands. This surprised no one; he had slept holding cars for as long as anyone could remember, so why not continue the habit for all future sleeps?

And after my year of 1988, I think I understand better. That familiar touch he was drawn to, echoing a lifetime of touches, unified his past with his present. Even if I started the year not knowing what I was wading into, by the end I can say I was doing something similar: gripping tight to what I once knew and taking it with me wherever I go next.

ADAM VAN WINKLE
Wrestling on TV, Wrestling with the Past

Grizzly Smith is no anomaly. Cook County Texas is full of drunks who can't show emotion beyond scorn and screwed. I wish I could say it was an honor, remarkable, to serve him beer at the Lakeway Beer Barn, the place I worked in high school, but truth is, he was the same as all the watery eyed sad sack Sunday drunks. He was so stooped that his legendary size was diminished, save his big floppy feet and hands. He didn't even have the big beard—it was more wisps of white hair clinging to his hollow cheeks. With his glasses he looked a lot like my stepdad.

Texoma, Texas ain't the roughest part of the country, but a hundred and fifty years ago, it was. And the great great great grandsons of the rough men of the past are still there. Back when, women and children were outlawed from running the streets at night it was such rough country. Back then, everything was named after animals and ideals.

Whitesboro over in Grayson County, where Grizzly was technically born, used to be "Wolf Path." Gainesville, the biggest town in Cook County where Grizzly had spent near all of his life, except of course when he was wrestling on the road, was first called "Liberty." Liberty, TX would be about fifteen miles west of Wolf Path, TX, as Gainesville is from Whitesboro today.

They lynched a Whitesboro man, a black man, named Abe Wildner, in the early 1900s, and there was a hard color line drawn between Grayson and Cook counties. Whitesboro outlawed black citizens. Gainesville did not. I grew up in Whitesboro.

Grizzly Smith's name was on the credits that rolled up the screen after WCW Saturday Night when I was a kid. He was "Assistant to Mr. Runnels." That means Dusty Rhodes, real name Virgil Runnels, hired him. Dusty Rhodes was the American Dream, the most popular wrestler from Texas not named von Erich. He'd hired our local Texan legend to work WCW.

I'd heard tell of Smith, and his sons, pro wrestler Jake Roberts and Sam Houston, how they were the local wrestling family. I watched tons of wrestling on television. Rented video tapes of old pay per views from the All-Star Video. Jake the Snake was one of my all-time favorites then. I always wanted Sam Houston to get over more than he did.

When my stepdad's drinking buddies heard I liked wrestling they were sure to note they knew the von Erichs, who were in Denton and Dallas, the big towns an hour away, and then they'd tell of Grizzly Smith and his sons growing up somewhere right around our little home area. My step-dad and his drinking buddies weren't that different from Grizzly Smith when I did meet, and serve, the man. They slurred these things at me with the same watery eyes he had. Sometimes they called me "queer" for liking to watch men wrestle on TV so much. My stepdad worried out loud a time or two that he was "afraid the boy might be gay."

I had a two-TV-rig in my room. Cable splitters are a wonder and when I figured out the mechanics of 'em around age eleven I crawled in the attic space of our brick ranch and split the cable line and run it down the inside of the wall of my room and punched it through so I could watch TV in my room. Mom controlled TV all night and my stepdad only liked Andy Griffith and Perry Mason. I had the little black and white TV from my stepdad's brokedown Chevy GoodTimes conversion van. Before it broke down and faded in the sun it was one of those decked out vans with drapes and swiveling chairs and space kids could run around before childseat laws, and this little TV. My other TV was scavenged from the Methodist Church Rummage Sale I was forced to volunteer at. It was a big wood consoled colored TV I got for ten bucks. I stuck another splitter on the cable end in my room and run both TVs—the little black and white stacked on top of the wood console TV.

Besides escaping my stepdad's drunk buddies and my parents' drunken sniping and fighting, my purpose was wrestling. WWF aired at the same time as WCW on Monday nights and now I could watch 'em both. Loved wrestling. Was hooked. Watched Saturday mornings and nights, Monday nights, Thursday nights, whenever. I didn't wanna miss a second.

I had my own storylines too. Wrestling characters I'd invent, insert into the storyline on TV. Choose sides. Invent finishing moves. Wrestle the pillows in my room. Had a big fat red beanbag chair for my room from the same church rummage sale. That was Yokozuna—sumo wrestler-cum-WWF champion. I body slammed him more than Lex Luger and Hulk Hogan combined. I was a glorious and celebrated champion.

Mom taught me to be such a vicious competitor, I'm sure of that. She made me physically tough. Hit me with a backhand, a board, a belt, what-ever it took to keep me in line. She assured me, even when I wasn't so sure, that I needed to be kept in line often. Sometimes she hit extra hard and I really don't think that was all me. Think that's because my stepdad didn't work and drank too much and sat around watching Andy Griffith instead of trying to find work during the day while Mom was working. At least I imagine that's why.

With both TVs on and me tossing the pillows and beanbag around, jumping from the top rope—the bed—and delivering a flying elbow deep into Yokozuna's throat--the noise of my parents fighting, or even just talking in that way, about my stepdad not working and drinking too much and sitting around watching Andy Griffith were not heard in my room. Ric Flair jawing back and forth with Sting on the microphone on WCW's Saturday Night grabbed me. Held me. Took me away. My parents arguing made me feel gnawing inside my stomach.

A pit hit my stomach at school one day too when Jared Patterson's notebook was discovered by some bully boys with a wrestling sketch in it.

He'd made a character. He called his wrestler "Firebird." I called myself, in my room arena, "Little Van Vader." Like I was Big Van Vader's son on account my name had "Van" in it too. They mocked Jared Patterson relentlessly. They called "Firebird" when he tried hard at anything, at school or at sports, made fun of him with it. Thank God I didn't make sketches in my notebook. Thank God I'd never let slip my secret wrestling identity, my prowess in the ring I imagined in my room. I couldn't have taken it all the way through school the way Patterson did.

A small circuit came through our little town when I was in eighth grade. I think it was called NCW and I imagine that stood for National Championship Wrestling. Local legend Jake the Snake Roberts was coming home, and he was going to fight the One Man Gang in the Whitesboro High School gym. Jake the Snake was way late. We waited an hour after the second to last match was done for Jake and Gang to get going.

When Jake, Grizzly's son, showed up finally, One Man Gang had to practically lay down for Jake to win as booked. Only after I had a few experiences of my own did I realize that what I saw that night was an extremely drunk and coked up man trying to wrestle.

Stopped following wrestling around the time I didn't have to be in my house anymore. Got a car. That was freedom. I could practically live in it and just sleep at home. Then went to college. I was gone.

In grad school a buddy showed me the glorious rabbitholes that exist in the internet space for behind the scenes info on all my favorite childhood wrestlers and storylines. I was hooked on wrestling again. Mind you, had no desire to watch it again, Monday nights. Don't need two TVs anymore. Just one screen with internet. And that's almost always wireless, no cables nor splitters required. Just comes to me.

I watched all about what became of Jake Roberts this way. Another son of a Texoma, Texas drunk. Documentaries got made tracking the spiral into drugs and redemption from addiction of Jake the Snake.

Before his recent recoveries Jake was terribly out of shape and an alcoholic. And, in *Beyond the Mat,* we learned the lengths and cause of his addictions as he scuttled for crack and told of his own conception when his father raped the teenage daughter of a lover. "He was born out of love...and I still love him," Grizzly Smith tells the camera in the next shot. I bet my stepdad that looked a little like Grizzly and drank just like him thought he called me a "queer" out of love.

My wife asked when we hit that space where we really loved each other and we could criticize each other how I could read so much about old wrestling and not care about watching it. I mean, think she's glad that I don't, but she was curious. And I thought about that too.

I mean it's interesting stuff. Think of your favorite childhood wrestlers and there's a good chance half of 'em are dead. Overdoses. Suicides. Cancer. Wrestlers are cursed, numbers support this. Big Van Vader, Macho Man, Mr. Perfect, Warrior, Rick Rude, Big Boss Man, Bam Bam

Bigelow—don't try to find them on the autograph circuit. Andre the Giant. He died young, but that's to be expected. And did you know Samuel Beckett used to give Andre the Giant who was a neighbor to Beckett in France rides to school so he didn't get made fun of on the bus for his size? Wikipedia is a glorious, glorious thing. Yokozuna, by the way, was dead before he was thirty-five of fluid on the lungs.

I think a lot about Jake Roberts. Probably knowing how flawed he is, and, growing up where he did, understanding some of where the voice and mannerisms and emotional vulnerability come from, knowing the kind of man he was raised by, I look to him as someone who had it stacked against him. Like me his parents were divorced. Like me, his dad was an alcoholic, passed on the addiction gene. Like me he was abused. Like me, he did enough dumb stuff that he might should be dead. Odds are he would be by now. Shockingly, we're still here.

Sometimes I think I may enjoy reading the behind the scenes stuff and watching the docs and clips now more than I enjoyed watching the wrestling on television then. As I've looked back and uncovered all the things of my childhood that were really going on, I find a lot of veils fall away. Like, what you thought was going on, what everyone was supposed to be working toward, that wasn't real. My mom and that stepdad divorced in my early twenties by the way. And this new wrestling hobby is really much the same. Same as growing up in the brick ranch where we all lived so unhappily, I'm fascinated by how it was really going down, the damage it did in the long run, the survivors and the dead.

TOM G. WOLF
Adventures in Paranormal Publishing

I have a distinct memory dating back to 1999, when I would have been thirteen or fourteen years old. I had just woken up, and I looked out of my bedroom window – something I did pretty much every morning as part of my routine.

Hovering over the next-door neighbour's backyard was a plain black helicopter, with no identifying markings or insignias. The volume should have been deafening, but there was no noise at all – the lack of sound was positively eerie. Dust and leaves should have been thrown up every-where, yet the ground beneath seemed to remain undisturbed.

I watched the helicopter hover for a while, then closed the curtains again, unsure of what to do. Was this the infamous Men in Black, lurking over my neighbourhood in one of their black helicopters?

Why had they come? Was it…was it for me?

This thought didn't perturb me as much as you might expect. After all, if the Men in Black were showing up, I was obviously getting close to The

Truth. The real secrets behind UFOs were within my reach.

Yet no black-suited figures exited the helicopter to harangue me; by the time I re-opened the curtains, the helicopter had gone, leaving no trace of its passage through suburbia.

I never saw it again.

*

A casual glance at the bookshelf in my office would raise an eyebrow among the more sober-minded. It's lined with a collection of various volumes about UFO sightings, alien abduction and related esoteric fare – paperbacks, hardbacks and magazines all slotted in comfortably next to one another. It's a collection that is the product of countless hours (and not inconsiderable funds) spent scouring second-hand bookstores across multiple countries, eBay and simply random chance.

I collect many things, but these books are arguably the collection I'm proudest of, and I am perpetually on the lookout for new additions to it. However, it's also been the one I'm most embarrassed about discussing with most friends and acquaintances. People will coo at the 2-foot tall Predator action figure, wax nostalgic at the sight of Lego or Transformers and let out a "fuck yeah!" at the heavy metal and horror posters. But the books about UFOs and aliens…well, they inspire a more mixed reaction.

So, to ask why I collect them at all would be a fair question. "Enjoyment" is the simple answer; to this day, if you give me a book on UFOs, a bowl of cheese rings and a beer, I will happily while away the whole afternoon.

But a lot of it can simply be attributed to my childhood surroundings; the bulk of my childhood was spent in the 90s, which was a wonderful time for anyone with even a modicum of interest in the idea of extraterrestrial life. Big hits in any form of media beget wider trends, and the enormous success of shows like *The X-Files, Unsolved Mysteries* and – here in Australia – *The Extraordinary* led to a huge upswing of public interest in UFOs and alien abduction. All manner of other paranormal phenomena was brought along for the ride too, and naturally publishing companies jumped onboard, pumping out thousands of volumes during the decade.

Of course, this newfound public interest itself didn't emerge fully-formed from the void. These shows were themselves an offshoot of a boom of interest in the subject during the 70s and 80s, thanks to books like Whitley Strieber's *Communion*. An ostensibly true account of Strieber's experiences with inhuman – possibly alien – intelligences, *Communion* sold a huge number of copies and helped solidify the image of the "Grey" among the general public. Time-Life's mail order series *Mysteries of the Unknown* was also prominent, even giving a young Julianne Moore one of her first acting roles in the accompanying TV commercials.

It can be traced back further too; the usual posited starting date is 1947, when Kenneth Arnold's strange sighting helped coin the term "flying saucer". Even this is overly reductive. But my larger point is that given that I grew up in a world where UFOs and aliens had a certain level of acceptance, if not approval. It's no surprise that I developed an interest in it.

Credit must also go to my father, who was and remains an incorrigible eccentric. When people share fond memories about their father, they often recite stories of the time their father took them to sport, read them bedtime stories or gave them a treat like ice cream. By contrast, one of my favourite memories of my father is the time he suggested that I give astral projection a try. The results themselves were unimpressive, but that was kind of beside the point.

Despite having become a fairly fervent Baptist in the 1970s (and endeavoured to raise his children in that tradition), he has maintained an interest in more…unusual…subjects to this day. He would likely credit this interest to his Scottish heritage – though it would not be unfair to point out that he grew up during the 60s and 70s, when the New Age movement was enjoying huge popularity, a sort of parallel to my own experience.

Naturally enough, UFOs, alien abduction and the paranormal became points of bonding for the two of us, from when I was probably 5 or 6 years old. We could talk for interminable periods about the subject, speculating as to the hows and the whys of alien life, whether it was visiting, its potential theological implications, and what it might mean for man's place in the universe. Even to this day he will ring me when he's stumbled across a new paranormal find in the second-hand bookstore or come across something at the library that might fit in among the other yellowed volumes in my collection.

The power of teenage loneliness probably played a role too. Though I had plenty of friends, I rarely hung out with them outside the confines of school. There was "nothing to do" at my place (though to be fair, you can extend that criticism to just about anywhere as a teenager), so I didn't invite people around. I didn't often take the initiative to go and hang out at a friend's place either. So, more often than not, solace was found in the confines of the local library. Open from 1-4 on a Sunday afternoon, it served as a haven against the loneliness that often plagues the final hours of the weekend – and that haven was oddly well-stocked with tales of extraterrestrial encounters.

With these kind of surroundings, Greys, Men in Black, black helicopters, horrific abduction experiences and mysterious lights in the sky all became regular fixtures on my mental landscape. And that's where I began to have some problems.

*

Having grown up to become a horror author, I now think my youthful obsession with UFO and alien abduction literature was just a manifestation of an interest in darker subject matter in general. It was a way for me to process feelings and urges which didn't necessarily have an effective outlet at the time. This would later take on a (mostly) healthier form as I embraced horror and heavy metal in my late teens. But when a childhood interest turns into a genuine obsession – as opposed to a strong fascination – issues can arise.

For me, the first signs of this came when I would have been about 10 years old. At the time, my family was living in a house which was relatively new but had numerous wiring issues. Light bulbs placed in my room didn't last for more than a week or two before blowing. The landlord was called, but no problem was evident, and so I ended up pretty much just relying on lamps and nightlights after that.

Today, this would be irritating and inconvenient, but not upsetting. But I suddenly began to have a ton of nightmares – night terrors, even. I had never really been a kid to be afraid of the dark, but I abruptly found myself terrified of it. I felt as though aliens were watching me and would come for me in my sleep if I let my guard down too much. I couldn't sleep properly and would often wake up sweating and terrified.

It's also no coincidence that this coincided with being accelerated at school, skipping ahead 2 years. A tall but slight kid, I suddenly found myself surrounded by kids who were hitting puberty and none too pleased at the idea of someone much younger than them outdoing them in class. It was my first and worst real-life encounter with bullying. Combine this with my reading material, and my real-life fears apparently found themselves processed through the night in a more bizarre way than I would have ever expected.

Fortunately, none of this lasted long. I ended up going back to my "real" year at school, and things had pretty much stopped by then anyway. I was able to slot back more or less into "normal" childhood and put my fears to one side. I still read such books occasionally, but they moved back into the realm of entertainment as opposed to canonical texts.

My second, more troubling bout came in 1999. I was in Year 8 at the time, and for the most part it was a good year at school. But I found myself menaced again by the fear of abduction. The night terrors weren't anywhere near as bad, but I frequently found myself gripped with anxiety for no particular reason. The underlying causes are far more mysterious to me than my earlier experience, but eventually culminated with the "encounter" with the black helicopter I mentioned back at the beginning.

It was traumatic and alien (ha!) to me, but after that occurred, things seemed to settle down a little. The absence of any further activity from outside forces helped me realise that my imagination was probably just getting a little overactive. I never sought any professional help, but I probably could have benefitted from some; but how do you explain these fears to someone who probably thinks the whole idea is bizarre or crazy to begin with?

*

Anyone who's engaged with the modern state of the UFO phenomenon will be well aware that the subject is often handled in a less than scientific manner. Anecdotal evidence is invoked as gospel, dubious means of memory recovery like hypnotism are widely used, and the surrounding field is rife with professional fraudsters, looking to score a few dollars from the gullible. Today, I sway to the disbelieving side of agnostic on the subject for all these reasons and more.

But twenty-odd years later, I still don't quite know what to make of that "memory" of the helicopter. The most likely explanation is that it's a conflation of dream, hypnopompic hallucination, the pressures of puberty and the influence of too many books about UFOs, with maybe a tiny trace of real memory in there…somewhere? Reading Jung as an adult helped contextualise it better for me personally; he saw UFOs largely as manifestations of the collective unconscious, symbols of a wholeness that we lacked in our lives. I am not sure that I agree with that explanation specifically, but it was a relief to read something like *Man and His Symbols* and come away knowing that my own experience was not particularly uncommon, nor necessarily something to be concerned about.

Whatever the original cause, this "memory" been solidified into its current memory by repeated retellings. I think the most practical lesson I can take from it as this point is an object lesson in the shortcomings of human recollection. It's also given me an increased sympathy (most of the time) for people who claim to have had some sort of unusual experience – even if nothing we might ordinarily recognise as "real" happened, it's still often a confronting or traumatic process for them.

Today, UFOs and aliens still lurk about my office, but largely on the printed page, as opposed to phantoms of the mind. It's a much healthier dynamic. Those books serve as relics of my childhood and teenage years, bits of publishing ephemera. They're also reminders of a time when high strangeness was simply part of the background noise – and the fun and dangers alike that it can bring.

Contributors

Dr. Benjamin Anthony currently practices on the shores of Lake Erie. His work has previously appeared with Gimmick Press, Clash Media, Gonzo Today, Graphic Policy and Nihilism Revised among other outlets. He can be found online at www.myfakehead.blogspot.com.

J. A. Bernstein is the author of a novel, *Rachel's Tomb*, which won the AWP Award Series and Hackney Prizes; and a chapbook, *Desert Castles*, which won the Wilhelmus Prize at *Southern Indiana Review*. His work has appeared in *Shenandoah*, *Tin House*, and *Kenyon Review Online*, among other places. A Chicago-native, he is an assistant professor of English at the University of Southern Mississippi and the fiction editor of *Tikkun*.

Michael Chin was born and raised in Utica, New York and currently lives in Las Vegas with his wife and son. He has three full-length short story collections on the way: *You Might Forget the Sky was Ever Blue* from Duck Lake Books, *Circus Folk* from Hoot 'n' Waddle, and *The Long Way Home* from Cowboy Jamboree Press. He has also published three chapbooks:

Autopsy and Everything After with The Florida Review, *Distance Traveled* with Bent Window Books, and *The Leo Burke Finish* with Gimmick Press. Find him online at miketchin.com and follow him on Twitter @miketchin.

Maggie Dove is a cross-genre Southern writer by way of Florida. Her work has appeared in *Hobart*, *JMWW*, and elsewhere.

Jacob Fowler (he/him/his) is an elementary school teacher living in Oakland, California. He recently graduated from Pitzer College with a BA in World Literature. His work has appeared in *Barren Magazine*, *Selcouth Station*, *Soft Cartel*, and *The Sunlight Press*, among others. You can find him on Twitter @jacobafowler.

Madeline Lane-McKinley is a founding editor of *Blind Field: A Journal of Cultural Inquiry*, a contributing editor at *Commune Magazine*, and the author of *Dear Z* (Commune Editions, 2019). She is a lecturer in Writing at the University of California, Santa Cruz, where she received her PhD in Literature in 2016. She lives in a collective house near the beach with her kid, partner, four friends, five dogs, and two cats.

Charles Austin Muir is the author of *This Is a Horror Book* and *Bodybuilding Spider Rangers and Other Stories*. His fiction has appeared in many anthologies of the dark and weird, including *Peel Back the Skin*, *Year's Best Hardcore Horror Vol. 1*, and *This Book Ain't Nuttin to Fuck With*. In a poll run by Silent Motorist Media, readers nominated him one of "Ten

Weird Writers to Save Us All in 2019." He lives in Portland, Oregon, with his wife, Kara--who is a competitive air guitarist--pugs, and a pit lab mix. His pop culture obsessions include Star Trek: TOS, 1980s Jane Seymour movies, and Debbie Gibson, of course.

Mark A. Nobles is a sixth generation Texan. Born on Fort Worth's infamous Jacksboro Highway, Mark proudly claims blood and kinship with Thunder Road's gamblers, outlaws, and wastrels. His work has appeared in or been published by *Cowboy Jamboree*, *Sleeping Panther Review*, *Crimson Streets*, *Cleaver Magazine*, *Curating Alexandria*, *The Dead Mule School of Southern Literature*, *Haunted MTL*, *Road Kill Vol. 4*, and other publications. He has produced and/or directed three feature documentaries and several short, experimental films. Mark lives in Fort Worth but hopes to die in the desert. He loves his two dogs, two daughters, and Texas, but not necessarily in that order. He can be found and followed on Facebook @ Flyin' Shoes Films.

Josh Olsen is a librarian in Flint, Michigan. He is the author of two books, *Six Months* (2011) and *Such a Good Boy* (2014), and he is the co-creator of Gimmick Press, along with his partner Katie MacDonald.

Matt Springer (@darthastuart on Twitter) is a fortysomething writer, father, husband and geek. By day, he markets and publicly relates; by night, he sleeps. He's published a collection of Star Wars essays entitled *Poodoo* and a novella entitled *Unconventional*, both available digitally.

Kyle Stedman (@kstedman on Twitter) is associate professor of English at Rockford University, where he teaches writing (creative, academic, professional, multimodal) and directs the writing center. He studies the rhetoric of sound and music, and he knows a lot about 1988.

Adam Van Winkle is the author of *Abraham Anyhow* (Red Dirt Press, 2017) and *While They were in the Field* (Red Dirt Press, 2019) and his stories have appeared in places like *Bull Men's Fiction, Red Dirt Journal, The Dead Mule School of Southern Literature, The Southern Literary Review, Cheap Pop, Pithead Chapel, Steel Toe Review, and Crack the Spine*. In addition to writing and editing grit lit he writes on wrestling for TWM News UK. Find him @gritvanwinkle.

Tom G. Wolf is a Sydney-based writer who specialises in pulp-style horror, UFO culture and heavy metal. By day he works as a journalist and copywriter. His work has appeared at *We Are the Mutants* and *Astral Noize*, and his horror novella, *Lost Tunnels*, can be purchased as an e-book on Amazon. He lives in Sydney with his wife and cat. You can follow him on Twitter: @lupinebookclub.

CPSIA information can be obtained
at www.ICGtesting.com
Printed in the USA
JSHW050852150920
7745JS00006B/79

9 781087 892863